SECRET ALASKA

A Guide to the Weird, Wonderful, and Obscure

Bailey Berg

REEDY PRESS

Reedy Press
PO Box 5131
St. Louis, MO 63139
reedypress.com

Library of Congress Control Number: 2024948770
ISBN: 9781681065830

Design by Jill Halpin

Unless otherwise indicated, all photos are courtesy of the author or in the public domain.

We (the publisher and the author) have done our best to provide the most accurate information available when this book was completed. However, we make no warranty, guarantee, or promise about the accuracy, completeness, or currency of the information provided, and we expressly disclaim all warranties, express or implied. Please note that attractions, company names, addresses, websites, and phone numbers are subject to change or closure, and this is outside of our control. We are not responsible for any loss, damage, injury, or inconvenience that may occur due to the use of this book. When exploring new destinations, please do your homework before you go. You are responsible for your own safety and health when using this book.

Printed in the United States of America
26 27 28 29   5 4 3 2

To the untamed wilderness of Alaska,
Where glaciers whisper ancient secrets,
Mountains stand as silent sentinels,
And the northern lights dance to a timeless rhythm.

To the people who call this rugged land home,
And to those who dare to explore its wild heart—
This book is for you.

Photo courtesy of National Park Service

CONTENTS

1 ... Introduction
2 ... Stubbs, Talkeetna's Fictitious Feline Mayor
4 ... Betting on Ice
6 ... White Alice
8 ... Sourdough
10 ... A MacGyvered Car
12 ... Spirit Houses
14 ... Alaska's Signature Beverage
16 ... Star, Anchorage's Unofficial Mascot
18 ... The Parking Fairies
20 ... Porta Potty Pushing
22 ... Of Bears and Salmon
24 ... Gold and Good Humor
26 ... On Dasher, On Dancer
28 ... Lend Me Some Sugar: I Am Your Neighbor
30 ... Roots Up
32 ... America's Last Whistle-Stop Train
34 ... A True Melting Pot
36 ... The Bar Fare of Choice
38 ... Dr. Seuss House
40 ... One Part Bar, One Part Museum
42 ... The Tale of Togo
44 ... A Village Frozen in Time
46 ... An Abandoned Mine
48 ... Shame on You
50 ... Alaska, Florida
52 ... Operation Breakthrough
54 ... Be Kind: Rewind
56 ... A Side of Ranch
58 ... Launched from the Sky on the Fourth of July

60 .... The Flower Man Lives On
62 .... Juneau's Most Famous Dog
64 .... A Remote Homestead
66 .... On the Half-Shell
68 .... It's Hammer Time
70 .... Eight Gold Stars in a Blue Sky
72 .... Sleeping Lady
74 .... Cowabunga, Dude
76 .... The Bawdy Past of Creek Street
78 .... All Aboard and Going Nowhere
80 .... Spinning a Yarn
82 .... An Unlikely Outpost
84 .... Hoot, Howl, Bugle, and Roar
86 .... Wilderness Woman
88 .... A Chocolate Cascade
90 .... Bunking Down in History
92 .... Ice, Ice Baby
94 .... Blue Babe
96 .... Here Comes the (Midnight) Sun
98 .... On the Rocks
100 .... World-Traveling Totems
102 .... The Only Way Out Is Through It
104 .... Beware the Crab
106 .... Four-Legged National Park Rangers
108 .... Cherry, Pumpkin, or Lemon Meringue
110 .... Hello, Dolly
112 .... Don't Forget Socks
114 .... Dollar Bills and Lime Wedges
116 .... Bus 142

118 .... A Town Built on Cheer
120 .... So Close, Yet So Far
122 .... A Lunar Landscape on Earth
124 .... Alaska's Favorite Cracker
126 .... An Architectural Oddity
128 .... There's Gold in Those Hills
130 .... Shake, Rattle, and Roll
132 .... Burning Man, Alaska Style
134 .... Cultural Preservation in a Modern Context
136 .... Up, Up, and Away
138 .... An Extra Serving of Vegetables
140 .... Fish On!
142 .... Nature's Light Show
144 .... In Celebration of Slush
146 .... Rudolph and All His Friends
148 .... Icy What You Did There
150 .... Alone in the Wilderness
152 .... Three Bears
154 .... Birds of a Feather
156 .... Flippers and Fins
158 .... Caribou and Sand Dunes
160 .... All Caught Up
162 .... Trusty *Tusty*
164 .... Stuck in the Middle
166 .... The Toughest 5K
168 .... Alaska's Two Elephants
171 .... Sources
179 .... Index

Northern Lights

INTRODUCTION

"There are strange things done in the midnight sun by the men who moil for gold . . ." So wrote Robert W. Service, the gold rush bard, in a poem included in his 1907 book *Songs of a Sourdough*. And more than 100 years later, the sentiment still rings true.

For centuries, a colorful cast of thrill-seekers, dreamers, and eccentrics have flocked to Alaska. They discovered what Indigenous peoples have known since time immemorial: This is a land where nature reigns supreme and humanity feels small. It is a place that has long offered a promise of opportunity, escape, self-discovery, and adventures far beyond the ordinary. Whether for the gold rush prospectors of the 19th century, the homesteaders of the 20th, or modern travelers seeking connection with the wild, Alaska continues to symbolize a place where extraordinary experiences aren't just possible—they're inevitable. You just have to be open to them.

With that in mind, this book is not about the Alaska you've seen on nature documentaries or tourist brochures. It's about the Alaska that hides in plain sight, a place brimming with the quirky, the bizarre, and, yes, the undeniably strange.

From remote ghost towns abandoned to time and the elements, to festivals where locals celebrate their love of outhouses, to the world's only hammer museum, this is a guide for the curious traveler seeking experiences that go outside the norm and for Alaska locals looking to learn more about the place they call home. We'll dive into the history of obscure local customs, meet the creatures whose legacies are etched into Alaska lore, and follow the stories of the characters who shaped this wild land in unusual ways. Welcome—and enjoy the journey.

STUBBS, TALKEETNA'S FICTITIOUS FELINE MAYOR

How did the nation come to believe a tabby cat had become the political leader of a small Alaska town?

For two decades, Talkeetna (population: roughly 1,000) was overseen by an unlikely political figure—one with whiskers, a tail, and a penchant for naps in the sun.

The politician in question was Stubbs, an orange tabby with an abbreviated tail. As a kitten, Stubbs garnered national attention when publications ranging from *The Washington Post* and *National Geographic* to CBS and NBC reported that the residents of Talkeetna, disillusioned with the human candidates running for mayor, decided to write Stubbs's name on the ballot as a form of protest.

However, that's not true. Talkeetna is a historic district and has never held an election. It's never had a mayor. If anything, Stubbs's "title" is an honorary one. And as to how the rumor started—and why so many national media outlets ran with it—nobody seems to know.

Still, Stubbs's story brought a steady stream of visitors to Talkeetna, many of whom made the journey specifically to meet the famous feline. His office was the local general store, Nagley's, where he could often be found lounging on the counter or, more frequently in the winter, enjoying the

NAGLEY'S STORE

WHAT: The Mayoral Office of Stubbs

WHERE: 13650 E Main St., Talkeetna

COST: Free to enter

PRO TIP: While Stubbs is gone, you can still see Aurora, who is considered the third honorary cat mayor of Talkeetna at Nagley's.

warmth behind the drinks cooler. If not at Nagley's, Stubbs might otherwise be found sitting on the bar in the adjoining West Rib Pub & Grill, lapping up catnip-laced water from a wine glass.

During his tenure, Stubbs used many of his nine lives. He was said to have survived BB gun shootings, a dog attack (that left him with a punctured lung, a fractured sternum, and deep lacerations), an accidental ride on a garbage truck, and a fall into a fryer (which, luckily, was turned off). It wasn't until July of 2017 that Stubbs passed away, simply because of old age. His people posted on his social media pages, "20+ years. Several uncontested elections. Thousands of naps. We had a good run."

Talkeetna, a small town in the shadow of Denali, is known for being quirky—it's the community that's said to have inspired the TV show *Northern Exposure*, after all.

BETTING ON ICE

What does a thawing river have to do with Alaska's only legal venue for gambling?

One of the longest continuously running betting events in the United States happens in a state where most forms of gambling, from slot machines to horse racing, have long been illegal. There's just one exception, and it involves wagering on when Alaska's long winter will end.

The rules are simple and haven't changed since the event's inception in 1917. On the first Saturday of March, a 26-foot-tall wooden tripod is embedded into the thick ice of the Tanana River, 300 feet from land, and hooked up to an antique clock in a watchtower on land using an elaborate rope-and-pulley system. When the ice on the river breaks up enough for the structure to travel 100 feet downstream, it triggers the clock to stop and a flood siren to blare. It's that exact time betmakers are trying to nail down. Choosing the right moment could result in a payout totaling hundreds of thousands of dollars.

Participants in the Nenana Ice Classic purchase tickets at $3 a pop to guess the exact date and time (to the closest minute) when the moving of the ice will freeze the clock. These tickets can be bought from the beginning of February through early April at one of the 200 or so gas stations, grocery stores, or bars throughout the state that are authorized retailers. At the end of the betting season, the wagers are rounded up and sent to Nenana by bush plane, train, car, and, in some cases,

---

The Nenana Ice Classic is an invaluable source of climate change data for scientists. Because there are so few variables, it's a highly accurate way to study how climate change has affected this remote part of Alaska.

Red buckets are scattered throughout Alaska to collect guesses.

Photos courtesy of Rebecca Troxel

dog sled. And each year, a crew of locals sorts through hundreds of thousands of tickets entirely by hand, which often means it's late into summer before a winner is announced. However, because there are so many guesses, there's typically more than one correct time. In 1973, for example, 58 people received a portion of the winnings. However, the 2014 jackpot netted the single winner more than $360,000.

THE NENANA ICE CLASSIC

WHAT: Yearly betting on the end of Alaska's winter weather

WHERE: Where the watchtower for the Nenana Ice Classic stands, 404 River Front St., Nenana

COST: Small fee to enter the contest; free to watch

PRO TIP: Each winter, the Nenana Ice Classic offers a live stream view of the Tanana River, so those who've wagered can keep an eye on the tripod.

WHITE ALICE

What does the Cold War have to do with Nomehenge?

Sitting atop Anvil Mountain in Nome, Alaska, are four white structures that, to the uninitiated, look like skateboarding half-pipes. Nicknamed "Nomehenge" or "the billboards," they sit atop the otherwise bald 1,200-foot mountain that serves as the backdrop for the town and are the remnants of a fascinating chapter of Cold War history.

NOMEHENGE

WHAT: Part of a Cold War–era communications network built against the ever-present threat of Soviet aggression

WHERE: Anvil Mountain Tower Rd., Nome

COST: Free to visit

PRO TIP: The hike from Nome to the antennas is particularly nice when fireweed is blooming in the summer.

In the 1950s, one of the US Air Force's primary goals was to build communications infrastructure in the vast, remote stretches of rural Alaska. The then territory's geographical position made it strategically important. However, it didn't have the roads, ports, and railroads needed to support defense missions. It also wasn't easy to alert those in the Lower 48 that Soviet bombers were headed toward the continental US to attack. If communities in rural Alaska had the ability to make long-distance phone calls, residents needed to make a reservation (and pay astronomical fees) to use the only circuit in town.

The White Alice Communications System, however, changed that.

The structures were tropospheric antennas and part of a vast network of 71 sites sprinkled throughout the state. The antennas worked by receiving radio waves from another White Alice site 200 miles away and hot-potatoing the missives down the line to the next remote site or military post by bouncing the dispatches off layers in the atmosphere. When the first

Roughly 80 tropospheric antennas were installed throughout Alaska as part of the White Alice Communications system during the 1950s. Photo courtesy of Casey Anderson

transmissions were made in January 1958, the tropospheric antennas were ahead of their time. Still, each site required teams of specialists constantly working to keep them running.

The sites were operational for about 20 years until advancements in satellite communications made them obsolete. After decommissioning, most were dismantled. However, in Nome, the legacy of the White Alice sites endures.

The strategic value of the White Alice Communications System helped boost Alaska's bid for statehood in 1959.

SOURDOUGH

What does a type of bread have to do with living in Alaska long-term?

One common nickname for longtime Alaska residents is "sourdough." It's a term that speaks to the endurance and spirit of the people who call this rugged region home.

The moniker finds its roots in the days of the early settlers and gold prospectors of the late 19th and early 20th centuries. During the Klondike Gold Rush, thousands of people ventured into the harsh and unforgiving landscapes of Alaska and the Yukon in search of fortune. In such an environment, resourcefulness was key to survival. A sourdough starter was one of the most valuable and versatile items that these early adventurers carried with them. This fermented mixture of flour and water, teeming with natural yeast and bacteria, was used to make bread and other baked goods.

"The Canadian Mounted Police refused to let any of the gold-seekers over the boundary at Chilkoot Pass [and into Alaska] without a year's supply of provisions," writes Ruth Allman, author of *Alaska Sourdough* (1976). "A 50-pound sack of flour—and a sourdough pot—would guarantee more satisfactory meals than canned food many times its weight."

Unlike commercial yeast, which was not available then, sourdough starter could be maintained indefinitely with proper care, providing a reliable means of leavening bread even in the most remote locations. Still, it had its challenges—prospectors

TALKEETNA ROADHOUSE

WHAT: Accommodations, a restaurant, and a café in a historic building

WHERE: 13550 E Main St., Talkeetna

COST: Varies

PRO TIP: Talkeetna Roadhouse makes pancakes and other baked goods from one of the oldest sourdough starters in the state—it's said to date back to 1902.

Above: *People outside of The Sourdough Hotel in Dexter, Alaska, in the early 1900s*

Left: *Talkeetna Roadhouse makes pancakes with their more than 100-year-old starter.*

were known to cuddle their sourdough at night to keep it from freezing. Being able to maintain sourdough was necessary for survival.

Over time, sourdough became a sobriquet for those who had proven their ability to endure and thrive in the challenging conditions of the North. It became a cultural badge of honor, a mark of respect and recognition for longtime residents who embody the resilience and tenacity that defined the early settlers.

The opposite of a "Sourdough" is a Cheechako. It's typically used for someone who just moved to Alaska and hasn't survived a full winter yet.

A MACGYVERED CAR

What was the one vehicle ever manufactured in Alaska?

The year was 1905 and 22-year-old Bobby Sheldon had a crush. The problem was, the object of his affection, a local woman in his hometown of Skagway, Alaska, was already seeing another man—one with an expensive horse and buggy. Sheldon figured his best bet for dazzling the lady was to up the ante with a vehicle. Because there weren't any cars in Alaska yet, Sheldon decided to build one himself.

The problem was, he'd never actually seen an automobile outside of magazine articles and newspaper clippings. No matter. He set about gathering the necessary scraps. The axles, metal wheels, springs, and chassis he pulled off an old porter cart. The seats had once been barstools. The hood was fashioned with scraps of tin, the steering lever was a gas pipe, and the headlights were made from two carbide mining lamps. For the engine, he salvaged a marine engine from a boat that had sunk in the harbor.

According to a *Fairbanks Daily News-Miner* article published in 1957, he took the woman on "many an exciting spin at 15 miles per hour" once the car was complete.

Sadly for Sheldon, the set of wheels wasn't enough to win the woman's heart. However, his fascination with automobiles did jump-start his career. In 1913, he became the first person

FOUNTAINHEAD ANTIQUE AUTO MUSEUM

WHAT: A collection of more than 100 ultra-rare vehicles, including the Sheldon

WHERE: 212 Wedgewood Dr., Fairbanks

COST: Fees vary for adults and children.

PRO TIP: Beyond the Sheldon, this museum has a slew of more than 100-year-old vehicles, including an 1899 Hertel Runabout and a 1921 Heine-Velox Victoria.

to drive a gasoline-powered car on the Valdez Trail, the only way to get from the port city of Valdez to Fairbanks, more than 360 miles away. After proving it was possible, he started a freighting business, helping people move to Alaska's remote interior, and later in life, he became the Alaska Road Commissioner.

The unique automobile is on long-term loan from the nearby University of Alaska's Museum of the North, another worthwhile spot to visit in Fairbanks, with more than 2,000 years of Indigenous art on display.

SPIRIT HOUSES

What happens when Russian Orthodox beliefs mix with Athabascan culture?

Thirty minutes outside of Anchorage, in a community known as Eklutna, is a graveyard where burial sites are topped with colorful, dollhouse-shaped structures. They are the product of cultural fusion.

Eklutna is considered one of the oldest continuous settlements of the Dena'ina Athabascan people in Alaska. For hundreds of years, it was just them. That was until the early 1800s, when Russian Orthodox missionaries arrived with a unique culture of their own. And over time, the two communities started to blend.

Until the arrival of the Russian Orthodox missionaries, the Dena'ina people cremated their deceased. The newcomers, however, strongly opposed the tradition. Because many of the Dena'ina converted to Russian Orthodoxy over the years, a compromise was made where they would bury their dead and erect houses over the burial places to protect the spirits from the elements and ensure they had a place to rest before making their final journeys to "the high country."

Traditionally, these houses are made of wood and painted in bright colors, often adorned with intricate patterns and designs. Each house is unique, reflecting the individuality of the deceased and the creator's artistic expression. The practice of building a spirit house begins shortly after a person's burial.

EKLUTNA HISTORICAL PARK

WHAT: A cemetery with colorful wooden houses as grave markers

WHERE: 26640 Eklutna Village Rd., Chugiak

COST: Free to visit

PRO TIP: You can also visit the old and new St. Nicholas Churches on either side of the cemetery.

The houses are often built by family members, allowing them to honor their loved ones while engaging in a therapeutic process of creation and remembrance.

Unlike gravesites elsewhere, these aren't tidied up when they fall into disrepair, as Athabascans believe anything taken from the earth must be allowed to return to it.

ALASKA'S SIGNATURE BEVERAGE

Would you drink something that had the word "fart" in the name?

What the rum runner cocktail is to Florida, the Sazerac is to New Orleans, and the cosmopolitan is to New York City, the duck fart is to Alaska.

Served as a layered shot and made with a half ounce each of Kahlúa, Baileys Irish Cream, and Crown Royal (in that order), it's potent, though it goes down easy, even when consumed in one gulp, as intended. It's much like a creamy coffee drink or a mudslide cocktail.

According to an *Anchorage Daily News* article from 1991, Dave Schmidt was tending an empty bar at the Peanut Farm on a snowy night in December 1987 when an elderly woman saddled up and ordered a shot of tequila, followed by a B-52 and then a grasshopper cocktail. Soon, the duo were experimenting with variations on classic beverages. At one point, Schmidt poured Kahlúa and Baileys into a glass, and the woman suggested adding a Crown Royal floater. It was an immediate hit.

While Schmidt told the newspaper he couldn't remember why he and his lone guest had settled on that name, it might have had something to do with the noise she made after

---

This classic Alaska cocktail is featured on the Discovery Channel's *The Deadliest Catch*. The day before the start of each crab fishing season, the captains gather to drink duck farts at a bar in Dutch Harbor.

Photos courtesy of Peanut Farm

downing the concoction—somewhat like a muffled belch that allegedly sounded like, well . . . a duck fart. Today the duck fart shot can be ordered anywhere throughout Alaska (or the world, for that matter).

PEANUT FARM

WHAT: A long-standing sports bar in Anchorage

WHERE: 5227 Old Seward Hwy., Anchorage

COST: Prices of food and drinks vary.

PRO TIP: If you want to get a duck fart from the source, go to the Peanut Farm.

STAR, ANCHORAGE'S UNOFFICIAL MASCOT

Why is there a reindeer in that downtown Anchorage home?

Among Anchorage's many attractions, one stands out as perhaps the most enchanting: Star the Reindeer, the city's unofficial live mascot.

Since 1960, a single reindeer has lived on the corner of Tenth Avenue and I Street in downtown Anchorage. The tradition started when Oro Stewart asked her husband, Ivan, if she could get an Alaskan pet. Thinking she meant a husky, he said yes. Instead, she came home with a female reindeer with a star-shaped white patch on its forehead.

Over the years, the Stewarts had five reindeer, each named Star because Oro wanted the local kids to always know who to say hello to. The first lived an uncommonly long 23 years (the average lifespan is just 15), though the second and third died young (the former having been stolen for food and the latter having accidentally eaten some plastic bags). The fourth lived to be 14, while the fifth died of a bacterial infection as a calf. When the Stewarts passed away themselves, it was assumed the tradition had gone with them—they'd received special permission to keep a reindeer in town. However, months later, when their friend Otto Whitehead was in the process

---

Alaska law states that non-Indigenous people are not allowed to own Alaskan reindeer. Even though Stars VI and VII were born at the Reindeer Farm in Palmer, Alaska, their parents were imported, so they've been considered Canadian reindeer by ancestry.

STAR THE REINDEER'S HOUSE

WHAT: A reindeer enclosure in downtown Anchorage

WHERE: 840 W 10th Ave., Anchorage

COST: Free to visit

PRO TIP: Star and his owner can often be spotted walking on downtown Anchorage's Delaney Park Strip.

of purchasing their home, he discovered a fortuitous loophole. The right to have a reindeer wasn't specifically given to the Stewarts but to the owners of the house. He could carry on the tradition.

Star the Sixth, whom Otto had for 15 years, was the most popular of the line—she was featured on National Geographic Wild and Animal Planet. Locally, she was known for accompanying her owner inside a downtown wine shop and to festivals like Fur Rendezvous. Otto adopted Star the Seventh in 2018, the first male reindeer in a 60-plus-year tradition.

THE PARKING FAIRIES

How do you stick it to parking meter monitors with humor?

For much of the '90s, sisters Susan and Linny Pacillo were known around Anchorage, Alaska, as the "Parking Fairies." After Linny received a $75 ticket because the previous owner of her new truck had put the renewal sticker on the wrong side of the plate, the sisters took it upon themselves to troll the overzealous parking enforcement patrol by cruising around downtown and filling people's meters while wearing tutus, wigs, and, of course, fairy wings.

The local civic heroes even went so far as to buy a Pepto-Bismol-pink 1973 Cushman (a small three-wheeled vehicle) so they could breeze past the foot patrol officers. Initially, they got locals to donate funds for the cause, but after a *USA Today* article about the sisters was published, donations came pouring in from across the country, and saving people from costlier tickets became a near full-time job. In 1994, the Parking Authority made $100,000 less than the previous year because of the Pacillos' efforts.

Assembly members tried to woo them, the Parking Authority tried to thwart them, but the sisters continued on until they won a ballot measure dismantling the Parking Authority.

THE LINNY PACILLO PARKING GARAGE

WHAT: A 10-story parking garage named for a woman who protested strict parking enforcement by paying other people's meters in a tutu

WHERE: 517 W 7th Ave., Anchorage

COST: Free to visit

PRO TIP: There is art throughout the garage, mostly inspired by Alaskan flora and fauna, but a piece in the main elevator lobby tells the Parking Fairies' story.

Left: *A mural of the Parking Fairies and their 1973 Cushman at the Linny Pacillo Parking Garage*

Above: *The Pacillo sisters and their 1973 Cushman. Photos courtesy of Susan Pacillo*

In 2006, Linny died after a battle with muscular dystrophy, and state legislators decided to dedicate a parking structure in downtown Anchorage in her memory. At the unveiling, they said it was because the "government needs to work for the people." In the years since, other cities across the US have seen their own "Parking Fairies" inspired by the Pacillos.

When the Parking Authority was finally dismantled in 1998, the Pacillo sisters celebrated by torching their fairy wings in a hot-pink burn barrel outside of Anchorage's City Hall.

PORTA POTTY PUSHING

What happens when you slap skis to the underside of an outhouse?

Hundreds of spectators line Fourth Avenue in downtown Anchorage, Alaska, on the last Saturday of February each year to cheer on the racers. It's not the Iditarod sled dogs—that event kicks off the following weekend—but this competition is also the biggest of its kind in the world.

It's the Outhouse Race.

Since 2006, dozens of teams have constructed an outhouse, affixed it to a pair of skis, and competed to see which group can push their commode down the road the fastest during the Fur Rendezvous festival.

There are no rules about what materials the portajohns can be built with, as long as they're structurally sound enough to last multiple heats. There are two categories teams can compete in: Traditional and Unlimited. For the former, the latrine needs to be a minimum of 30 inches by 30 inches and have three walls, while the latter can be as large as 12 feet long and 8 feet wide and tall.

THE OUTHOUSE RACE

WHAT: A world-famous sprint with toilets

WHERE: 4th Ave. (between E and F Sts.), Anchorage

COST: Free to watch; fee applies to compete

PRO TIP: Just like in the Iditarod, a Red Lantern is awarded to the slowest team.

The Unlimited class is also known as the "honey bucket" round, and often you'll see just a five-gallon plastic bucket on skis. It pokes fun at how long it took Alaska to get indoor plumbing.

Regardless of the bracket, all must contain a toilet seat and a roll of TP. During the race, there must be one helmeted (this event can get pretty rowdy) rider and a maximum of four pushers and pullers.

Even those who aren't the fastest can win other titles: Best Theme (TARDIS and mailboxes to Santa have been popular outhouse themes in the past), Most Realistic, People's Choice, and Cleanest, to name a few. The trophy? A toilet paper holder, of course.

OF BEARS AND SALMON

Who's the fattest bear at Katmai National Park?

Spanning 4 million acres on a remote island in Alaska's Aleutian Chain, Katmai National Park is best known for one thing: bears.

It's one of the best places in the world to see brown bears in their natural habitat because it's so densely populated with the predators—it's estimated that more than 2,200 of the bruins live there.

Their population is so bountiful thanks to the sheer number of salmon that charge upstream. Between June and September each year, hundreds of thousands of sockeye salmon leave the ocean and follow their internal homing devices up the Brooks River to return to the very spot they came into the world. There, they'll spawn (or fertilize) their own eggs and die, completing their life cycle. That is if they can hurl themselves over Brooks Falls, a six-foot-tall waterfall within the preserve, and not get caught in the gaping maw of one of the waiting ursids.

Those silvery fish are a 4,500-calorie bomb, meaning the bears put on a lot of heft each summer—the park estimates each bear packs on more than two pounds a day, helping them build up their fat reserves for hibernation. Enthusiasts can watch the corpulent carnivores all summer from their homes, thanks to explore.org, an animal webcam site that sets up cameras each season to livestream the bears 24/7. Then, each

---

Katmai was established in 1918 to protect the Valley of Ten Thousand Smokes, a landscape that looks so post-apocalyptic—with smoking valleys, steam vents, and lava flows—that NASA's *Apollo* astronauts used the site in the mid-'60s for training. They believed it was a good representation of the moon.

fall before the bears tuck in for their winter slumber, the public can throw their weight behind what they consider the chunkiest bears, voting on the pantheon of pudge in a wildly popular single-elimination bracket-style contest on the website.

BROOKS CAMP

WHAT: A visitor site close to Brooks Falls, one of the most popular viewing spots for brown bears in the protected land

WHERE: Katmai National Park, King Salmon

COST: No entrance fee

PRO TIP: In peak season, as many as 50 bears wait on the lip of the falls at any given time, and an estimated 300 salmon may attempt the leap every minute, making it an incredible photo opportunity.

Photos courtesy of National Park Service

GOLD AND GOOD HUMOR

How did a gold rush town get a feathered name?

Nestled in the rugged wilderness of eastern Alaska is a small, unincorporated community with a unique name: Chicken.

During the gold rush era of the late 1890s, prospectors flocked to the area in search of fortune and eventually formed a town. Per a 1942 *Anchorage Daily Times* article, "The government gave them a post office and told them to name it. Because there were so many ptarmigans there, they decided to name it Ptarmigan. But when it came right down to it, no one knew how to spell the word, so they said: 'Oh, we might as well call it Chicken and be done with it.'"

While the story of illiterate prospectors and a fowl spelling error is funny, it may not be true. In fact, a 2024 *Anchorage Daily News* article argued as much, adding that the oldest relevant source that may point to the true origin story is an 1898 US Geological Survey report on the nearby Chicken Creek that read, "The creek is so named from the size of the gold, which is about that of chicken feed (corn)."

Not knowing which (if either) tale is true hardly seems to ruffle any feathers of the dozen residents of Chicken. One

---

In the 1950s, just before statehood, many communities vied to be the capital. State Representative Bob McCombe, a resident of Chicken, offered his town, including 1,700 acres of land, as the new site in 1959. He told the *Fairbanks Daily News-Miner*, "If that offer isn't enough land, we'll offer more. We're not Chicken."

"Downtown" Chicken, Alaska. Photos courtesy of Douglas DeVore

CHICKEN GOLD CAMP & OUTPOST

WHAT: A historic site that offers a glimpse into the town's gold mining past.

WHERE: Airport Rd., Chicken

COST: Free to visit

PRO TIP: You can try your hand panning for gold nuggets on one of the Gold Camp claims.

of the town's most endearing aspects is its embrace of the quirky name—the community proudly displays chicken-themed decorations throughout town, including a massive metal chicken made from recycled school lockers named Eggee, who roosts on a hill overlooking the Pedro Dredge at Chicken Gold Camp.

ON DASHER, ON DANCER

Do you think you can outrun a reindeer?

On the first Saturday of March, after the famed Iditarod Sled Dog Race has started and all the teams of dogs have set off for Nome, hundreds of Alaskans take their mark in the middle of downtown Anchorage's main street for another race: the Running of the Reindeer.

The annual event is this city's version of Pamplona's running of the bulls. However, it's not as treacherous as the Spanish event it is styled after. Each year, there are four heats—one for men, one for women, one for teams, and one for tourists—where, after the starting gun goes off, racers make a three-block dash down the snow-covered Fourth Avenue. After the two-legged runners are given a healthy head start, the four-legged (and antlered) ones are let loose. There have never been collisions—at least not

RUNNING OF THE REINDEER

WHAT: A footrace against real, live reindeer

WHERE: 4th Ave. (between D and H Sts.), Anchorage

COST: Entry fee for runners; free for spectators

PRO TIP: If you want to watch the races, get there early—it's a popular event and short people especially might have a hard time finding a viewing spot.

Costumes are common at the Running of the Reindeer—some of the most popular get-ups include carrots (a favorite snack of reindeer) and bull's-eyes.

with the reindeer (though runners who have indulged in a pre-race pub crawl and crashed into one another are another matter). Reindeer hate having their antlers touched and are incredibly agile, so they bob and weave through the crowds effortlessly. And they always make it to the finish line first.

The animals aren't running in pursuit—they're running to the handful of reindeer being held near the finish line. To reindeer, home is where the herd is, so they instinctively run to get back to each other.

The event has been running since 2008, and each year, proceeds are donated to Toys for Tots.

LEND ME SOME SUGAR: I AM YOUR NEIGHBOR

How do you squeeze an entire town under one roof?

Wedged between Prince William Sound and the Chugach Mountains is a long, skinny sliver of land known as Whittier. Encompassing just over 12 square miles, the only way to get there is on a boat or through a single-lane, 2.5-mile-long toll tunnel burrowed through Maynard Mountain.

While there are myriad hard-to-reach communities in Alaska (in fact, there are roughly 200 that don't have roads to them at all), what makes Whittier unique among fairly inaccessible towns is that almost all of the roughly 280 year-round residents live under one roof. That building is the Begich Towers Condominium, a 14-story apartment complex with 150 two- or three-bedroom units. It also contains the town's only grocery store, church, post office, community center, health clinic, and police station. Those who don't live in Begich Towers reside in another,

KOZY KORNER

WHAT: The only grocery store in Whittier

WHERE: 100 Kenai St., Whittier

COST: Prices vary

PRO TIP: You'll find Kozy Korner on the ground level—though be prepared to pay a premium.

There's another condo building in Whittier, the Buckner Building, which was built in the 1950s to house military personnel. Beyond apartments, it held a bowling alley, a movie theater, and a pool, though it was eventually abandoned.

smaller, two-story condo building known as Whittier Manor—there are no single-family homes in Whittier.

The town was established in the early 1940s as a railway hub and military port known as Camp Sullivan. The ice-free port and location, which is relatively protected from enemy attacks, was of significant strategic value. Begich Towers, built in 1956, was meant to house military officers, soldiers, and dependents. However, in the '70s the military withdrew, and Begich Towers transitioned to civilian accommodations.

The big reason why there aren't more lodging options is that what little area is left of the town is mainly tidal areas and vertical rock faces—there just aren't alternative places to build. Though given how variable the weather in Whittier is, with wind gusts up to 60 miles per hour and upwards of 200 inches of rain and 250 inches of snow per year, it makes sense that the city is largely confined to one building—nobody has to brave the elements to run errands.

Most of the town of Whittier lives in Begich Towers.

ROOTS UP

How do you get an upside-down tree?

Tucked inside Tongass National Forest, this botanical garden has a unusual claim to fame: trees are upside-down.

After a landslide uprooted much of Thunder Mountain's vegetation in 1985, locals Steve and Cindy Bowhay bought the tract of land and set about restoring it. The story goes that while working on reviving a stream, Steve accidentally damaged a piece of machinery and, in his frustration, used the machine to pick up a fallen tree and slammed it upside-down into the mud. He liked the look of it and decided to repeat the action with more than two dozen other trees, later using the root balls as natural planters.

Now known as "Flower Towers," the gnarled root balls form a cradle, and with the help of netting and mosses to fill in the gaps, the owners are able to plant an array of riotously colorful trailing flowers, like begonias, petunias, and rhododendrons, in the natural planters each year.

GLACIER GARDENS RAINFOREST ADVENTURE

WHAT: A one-of-a-kind botanical garden

WHERE: 7600 Glacier Hwy., Juneau

COST: Fee varies for adults and children.

PRO TIP: Located on Thunder Mountain, this garden has one of the best panoramic views of Juneau.

Beyond the Flower Towers, guests can see manicured gardens, old-growth rainforest, and an active bald eagle nest while on the tour at Glacier Gardens Rainforest Adventure.

Photo courtesy of Jennifer Nielsen Johnson

Today you can visit on a guided tour. After you've pondered the mystery of the Flower Towers, you can visit the 50 acres of giant spruce and hemlock trees in the surrounding temperate rainforest and learn about other Alaska flora, like the prickly Devil's Club and fireweed.

AMERICA'S LAST WHISTLE-STOP TRAIN

How do you stop a locomotive in its tracks?

For more than 100 years, the Alaska Railroad has connected Seward, a small port community on the southern coast of the Kenai Peninsula, to Fairbanks, an interior city nearly 500 miles north. The government initially built the railroad as a way to move troops and precious metals throughout the then-territory. However, today it's more commonly used to shuttle

---

> The Alaska Railroad predates many of the communities it now stops in—Anchorage, for example, was formed as a tent city to support the railway's construction.

tourists throughout southcentral Alaska—more than half a million people ride at least one of the five main routes each year.

The Alaska Railroad also operates the last whistle-stop route in the country. Would-be riders need only stand near the track and extend their thumb or wave a piece of fabric to get the midnight-blue-and-gold-painted locomotive to stop and let them on board. The service is available on a 150-mile stretch of track between Talkeetna, a town that frequently serves as a jumping-off point for mountaineers climbing Denali, and the Hurricane Gulch Bridge, a 918-foot-long steel-arch platform suspended nearly 300 feet above its namesake gulch and the fast-moving Chulitna River with spectacular views of the surrounding wilderness.

The whistle-stop service is primarily used by rugged adventurers looking to fish, hunt, or camp in the Indian River Valley and homesteaders who live off the grid in this remote, roadless section of the state. For the latter, the train serves as an essential lifeline to get to bigger cities when they need to and to learn news of the world, as there often isn't cell phone coverage or Wi-Fi in this region.

An Alaska Railroad train pulling out of Talkeetna

ANCHORAGE DEPOT

WHAT: The railroad station at the center of the Alaska Railroad system

WHERE: 411 W 1st Ave., Anchorage

COST: Free to visit; price of train ride varies by route.

PRO TIP: On the train, opt for the more upscale GoldStar Class—it has second-floor seating and picture windows to better see animals.

A TRUE MELTING POT

What makes Anchorage the most diverse city in the nation?

Alaska has long been a north star for immigrants, refugees, and those from the contiguous US looking to start anew. It's hard to say why: It may be because it's a younger state with more room for newcomers to try new ventures, or it may be because Alaska just has a reputation for those looking for an adventure. To that point, roughly 11 percent of people in Anchorage, the most populous city, were born in another country, and another 47 percent were born in another state, according to the most recent census data.

It might also come as a surprise to learn that the Anchorage metro area has a population of just under 300,000 people, yet it contains the three most diverse neighborhoods (Mountain View, Airport Heights, and Fairview) in all of the United States.

According to sociologist and demographer Dr. Chad Farrell, what makes Anchorage so diverse is a near equal split within many neighborhoods of the seven race groups recognized by Farrell's study (White, Black, Latinx, American Indian and Alaska Native, Asian, Native Hawaiian and Pacific Islander, and biracial). No group is significantly more represented than another. It also means the city has no Little Italys, Chinatowns, or other ethnic enclaves—the community is well blended. Similarly, Anchorage holds 19 of the top 20 most diverse elementary schools in the nation (the one

NEW SAGAYA CITY MARKET

WHAT: A specialty grocer with foodstuffs from around the world

WHERE: 900 W 13th Ave., Anchorage

COST: Varies

PRO TIP: The deli offers myriad hot and cold entrées, many with Asian and Pacific Island origins.

Downtown Anchorage seen from Earthquake Park

outstanding being in Honolulu). It's estimated that more than 100 languages are spoken in the homes of the roughly 44,000 students in the district, ranging from Ukranian and Samoan to Hmong and Yup'ik (a language spoken by Alaska Natives in southwestern and western Alaska).

Anchorage's diversity means that there are oodles of incredible restaurants throughout town with cuisines spanning the globe.

THE BAR FARE OF CHOICE

Do you want Coca-Cola-glazed onions with that?

Moose, caribou, bear, and Dall sheep all roam across the 49th state, but you won't find them on restaurant menus. Because they are protein sources Alaska Natives have traditionally harvested, they're considered subsistence foods and therefore cannot be commercially sold.

The one big-game meat exception is reindeer. That is because they are technically domesticated animals (the wild ones are caribou), while the others live freely. You'll find reindeer as a pizza topping, simmered in soups, and stuffed into omelets and breakfast burritos throughout Alaska. However, arguably the most popular preparation is in hot dog form. Butterflied and seared on a food cart flat-top grill, the frankfurters are served on a toasted bun with customers' choice of ketchup, mustard, relish, sauerkraut, cheese, jalapeños, and Coca-Cola-glazed onions. And while they're available throughout the day, especially in

TIA'S GOURMET SAUSAGES AND HOTDOGS

WHAT: One of the oldest operating link stands in Anchorage

WHERE: 573 W 4th Ave., Anchorage

COST: Varies

PRO TIP: Be sure to get the spicy reindeer dog.

In case you were curious, reindeer tastes like a milder form of venison. The hot dogs are typically blended with pork or beef, too.

the summer, the lines for these delicacies are longest around bar close, especially in larger cities like Anchorage and Fairbanks. There's something so satisfying about the snap of the casing when bitten into after a couple of rounds of beverages. However, if you can't stomach the idea of ingesting Rudolph, the stands typically offer brats, Louisiana hot links, Italian sausages, and all-beef hot dogs, too. Though, to be fair, because of the high cost of reindeer meat, the hot dogs are a blend of proteins.

DR. SEUSS HOUSE

What would you do to ensure your view of North America's highest mountain was never blocked by trees?

Tucked into the Alaskan wilderness between the small towns of Willow and Talkeetna stands a whimsical architectural marvel known officially as the Goose Creek Tower and colloquially as the "Dr. Seuss House." The latter sobriquet is because this peculiar structure often draws comparisons to the fantastical illustrations found in the beloved children's books.

Construction of the eclectic building started in the late '90s, shortly after an Alaskan lawyer named Philip Weidner bought the land. Initially, he intended to build a simple two-story cabin. However, as Weidner's imagination took flight, the modest cabin quickly evolved into a tower consisting of a series of increasingly smaller cabins stacked one on top of the other. All told, it stands 185 feet tall, and depending on how you look at it and which staircases you climb to the top, there are between 14 and 17 stories. Though

ALASKA RAILROAD DEPOT, TALKEETNA

WHAT: The closest railway depot to the Goose Creek Tower

WHERE: 22889 S Royal Blue Loop, Talkeetna

COST: Train ticket prices vary.

PRO TIP: The Denali Star Train passes the Dr. Seuss House in the summer, while the Aurora Winter Train rolls by in the winter.

For the best view of the Dr. Seuss House, consider taking a flightseeing trip out of Talkeetna—often the pilots will ask if you want to do an aerial drive-by for a better look.

Photo courtesy of Shane Parker

don't expect it to get any taller now—200 feet is officially federal air space, so the owner doesn't plan to go any higher.

The building is privately owned, and while the owner had previously said he'll offer tours when it's done, it's still a construction zone, so it's not safe to enter. However, it's possible to see the house on the train heading north, as well as on some spots on the Parks Highway.

ONE PART BAR, ONE PART MUSEUM

How did an Anchorage dive get named the number one bar in America?

Walking into Chilkoot Charlie's (known simply as Koot's to locals) often feels like stepping into the pages of an *I Spy* book. Wandering around the many rooms, you might find a life-size replica of the *Sputnik* satellite, a framed *Playboy Magazine* article from 2000 naming Koot's the best bar in America, a chunk of the Berlin Wall, a taxidermied king crab, and a newspaper clipping with a headline from when Alaska achieved statehood that reads, "Ike says: you're in now."

When Koot's opened in 1970, it was a one-room dive bar in the heart of Anchorage's historic Spenard neighborhood, with sawdust floors, padded beer kegs for seating, and cheap drinks. It's still that, but since then nine additional bars have been built onto it, each with their own unique theme. The Ice Bar features a bar top constructed out of 25 feet of solid ice. Then there's the Bird House, an exact replica of another

CHILKOOT CHARLIE'S

WHAT: An institution in the Alaska bar scene

WHERE: 2435 Spenard Rd., Anchorage

COST: Varies

PRO TIP: Most of the bars don't open until after 9 p.m., so plan on coming late.

Some big national acts have shaken the walls of Chilkoot Charlie's over the years, ranging from Lynyrd Skynyrd and Metallica to Green Day and the Doobie Brothers.

local bar that burned down and was known for having a ceiling papered with business cards and panties. Perhaps most bizarre is the Russian Room, which takes up most of the second floor and is a reproduction of a tsarist-era ballroom, complete with onion domes and latticed windows. There are display cases with Russian porcelain eggs that date back to the 1890s, hundreds of medals given to civilians by Soviet leaders (including "Valor in Childbearing, Second Class," given to women who had more than seven children), a massive portrait of the Romanov family, Soviet hockey pins, a 17th-century Russian Orthodox cross, military uniforms, and more.

THE TALE OF TOGO

Who is the real hero of the serum run?

Isolated from the outside world, Nome, a community situated on the Bering Sea in western Alaska, entered the nation's collective consciousness in 1925 when a deadly diphtheria outbreak threatened to level the town. Inaccessible by ship due to thick winter ice, the only way to get the lifesaving serum to the far-flung community was by dog sled.

In a relay race against time, 20 mushers and roughly 150 dogs crossed nearly 700 miles through whiteout conditions, over rivers of splintering ice, and against howling winds that dropped the wind chill to minus 85 degrees Fahrenheit to deliver the antitoxin.

The story of their success elevated the profiles of two mushers, Gunnar Kaasen and Leonhard Seppala, and their dogs. Afterward, they toured the US, meeting fans and appearing in ad campaigns. However, one pup received an extra large serving of fame: Balto. As the lead dog in Kaasen's team (though owned by Seppala), Balto was the first to charge into Nome. He was immortalized with a statue in New York City's Central Park and appeared in a number of movies.

However, Balto only ran 55 miles, while Togo, Seppala's lead dog, guided his team through the most dangerous terrain of the trail, covering 261 miles, roughly five times the distance of the other teams. Many Alaskans argue that Togo was the true hero of the serum run.

THE IDITAROD TRAIL SLED DOG RACE HEADQUARTERS

WHAT: Where Togo lives on

WHERE: 2100 S Knik Goose Bay Rd., Wasilla

COST: Free

PRO TIP: After Togo's death, his owner had him preserved and mounted—he's now on display at the Iditarod Headquarters.

Togo (farthest left) and some of the other sled dogs on his team. Photos courtesy of Carrie M. McLain Memorial Museum

In 1960, 31 years after Togo's death, Seppala said, "I never had a better dog than Togo. His stamina, loyalty, and intelligence could not be improved upon. Togo was the best dog that ever traveled the Alaska trail."

In 2019, Disney released a film adaption of Togo's story—the dog actor who portrayed the famous pooch was a direct descendant of Togo, 14 generations back.

A VILLAGE FROZEN IN TIME

How do you keep a culture the same for more than 300 years?

Here's how Nikolaevsk, a village just 10 miles off the busy Sterling Highway and sandwiched between prolific salmon and halibut fishing towns, became one of the largest communities in the world of a particularly stringent offshoot of the Russian Orthodox Church, started in 1666.

The Church had just made some fairly minor reforms (including using three fingers instead of two when making the sign of the cross) that didn't sit well with some of the congregants, so they decided to break off from the church and continue observing their religion as they always had, styling themselves as Russian Old Believers. Because the state wouldn't allow them to just agree to disagree, those who wouldn't practice in secret were forced to flee to Siberia. Then, in the early 1900s, the Communist revolution drove them to China, where they survived by hunting tigers and elk until just after World War II when China kicked out all foreigners. Eventually, the former Russians settled in the former Russian territory of Alaska.

Though not far from several bigger Alaskan cities, the Russian Old Believers still try to live a traditional life: They wear colorful embroidered outfits with handwoven belts,

Before settling in Alaska, the Russian Old Believers tried Brazil and Oregon. The former they deemed too hot, while the latter was too close to big, modern cities they worried would corrupt the youth.

students speak both English and Russian, and signs held up at football games often use the Cyrillic alphabet.

The town really has only one business open to outsiders: a small restaurant called Samovar Cafe run by a septuagenarian babushka. There, the proprietor pumps customers from around the world full of traditional Russian foods and has a knack for dressing them to look like life-size Matryoshka dolls for a hefty fee. It's a dizzying, wallet-lightning experience to be sure but also a rare look into a community that doesn't often throw open its doors to visitors.

SAMOVAR CAFE

WHAT: The only business open to outsiders in Nikolaevsk (though hours are inconsistent)

WHERE: 64935 Nikolaevsk Road, Nikolaevsk

COST: Varies

PRO TIP: Get the borscht and be careful of the upsell. Across from the courthouse.

Photo courtesy of Bill Herndon, Flickr

AN ABANDONED MINE

How did Kennicott go from thriving mining community to ghost town in a generation?

First explored by a pair of prospectors in the summer of 1900, Kennicott was established as a mining community in 1903. From there, it blossomed. At its peak, it was home to more than 600 miners who pumped out copper ore around the clock. In just over 30 years, the workers had dug up around $200 million of the precious metal from the surrounding mountains. But when the ore deposits were depleted, the mines closed. By 1938, Kennicott became a ghost town.

For decades, the mill sat empty and abandoned. Then, in 1998, the National Park Service purchased from private owners the mill, power plant, and many other camp buildings, ranging from sun-bleached shops to weather-worn bunkhouses, and began restoring them.

Now visitors can take a tour of the mill, a fire-engine-red 14-story behemoth that was used to process the ore, with one of the national park rangers—it is worth it for the glaciers and mountain views from the top floors and the opportunity to check out the massive more than 100-year-old machinery. There's also oodles of information about the history of the mines and the people who once worked there at the Kennecott Visitor Center and the original General Manager's Office. The Blackburn School, Recreation Hall, Refrigeration Plant, Railroad Depot, and Power Plant are all open for visitors, too.

KENNECOTT MINES NATIONAL HISTORIC LANDMARK

WHAT: Ghost town within Wrangell-St. Elias National Park

WHERE: Kennicott, Chitina

COST: Free to visit

PRO TIP: Be sure to visit the exhibits in the old General Store and Post Office.

The reason Kennecott Mines is spelled with an "e" and the community of Kennicott uses an "i" is because of a clerical error on the original official paperwork.

SHAME ON YOU

How far would you go to see a wrong righted?

In the days before courtrooms, when Indigenous Alaskans were wronged (like someone refusing to pay their debt, for example), they commissioned a shame pole. A type of totem pole, it would bear the likeness of the wrongdoer (and the story of what happened) and was placed in a prominent place to embarrass the offender. The public ridicule usually worked. When he or she righted the wrong, the pole was taken down and the story was not told again.

One of the most famous was erected in Saxman, near Ketchikan, in the 1880s to ridicule William H. Seward, the secretary of state who orchestrated the purchase of Alaska from Russia. Not only did the politician ignore the claims of Indigenous people to the lands he oversaw the sale of, but he also failed to repay the generosity of Chief Ebbits, a tribal leader who welcomed Seward with a lavish gift-giving feast known as a potlatch. By 2014, the pole had started to deteriorate, and because the debt hadn't been resolved, the City of Saxman commissioned a reproduction by artist Stephen Jackson.

SAXMAN TOTEM PARK

WHAT: Two dozen totem poles, including the Seward Shame Pole

WHERE: 2660 Killer Whale Ave., Saxman

COST: Small fee to visit

PRO TIP: Be sure to visit the carving shed to see what master carvers are working on now.

Carved of red cedar, totem poles have traditionally been used to document stories and histories important to local families or communities.

A shame pole bearing the likeness of William H. Seward in Saxman, Alaska

Shame poles are still used today, though to a lesser extent. In 2008, Cordova-based artist Mike Webber made a shame pole aimed at ExxonMobil, saying that they didn't live up to the promises they made following the *Exxon Valdez* oil spill. Similarly, in 2019, Sitka-based artist Tommy Joseph erected a shame pole targeting Alaska's elected leadership (and then-President Trump), whose policies he believed were gutting Alaska.

ALASKA, FLORIDA

What does an old-school dessert have to do with Alaska?

Baked Alaska, a dessert consisting of sponge cake, ice cream, and toasted meringue, is hard to find in much of the world unless you're looking in dusty old cookbooks. It's not an easy treat to prepare and has somewhat fallen out of fashion.

The story of how Baked Alaska came to be is also heavily debated. Some accounts say a version of the treat first appeared in 1802, with Thomas Jefferson serving ice cream encased in a hot pastry at a state banquet. In the 1830s, European diners were introduced to the very similar "Norwegian omelette." However, the most commonly accepted tale is that it was invented in 1867 at Delmonico's, an upscale steakhouse in New York City, by French chef Charles Ranhofer, either to make fun of or to celebrate the Alaska Purchase. Delmonico's version called upon banana ice cream and walnut spice cake enrobed in meringue torched to a golden brown, originally called Alaska, Florida, a nod to the juxtaposition of the hot and cold components. When it was renamed Baked Alaska, nobody knows for sure.

WILD SCOOPS TEST KITCHEN

WHAT: A small-batch ice cream shop with a Baked Alaska twist

WHERE: 530 E Benson Blvd., Anchorage

COST: Varies

PRO TIP: While any flavor ice cream can be made into a version of Baked Alaska, for a more authentic take, opt for one with cake bits swirled in.

Whatever its origins, in Alaska, the eponymously named sweet is making a comeback, albeit with a twist. In recent years, more eateries in the state have been experimenting with their own versions of the more than 150-year-old recipe. Two Anchorage examples are found at Whiskey & Ramen (which incorporates miso) and the ice creamery Wild Scoops (they top their ice cream with torched marshmallows).

Meringue is a good nonconductor of heat, allowing it to protect the ice cream for a minute or two while it is browned.

OPERATION BREAKTHROUGH

How did a rescue of three whales help lead to rare collaboration between the US and the Soviet Union?

Located along the Arctic Ocean's icy shores, Utqiagvik made national news in October 1988 after a local hunter found three juvenile gray whales trapped in winter sea ice near town. The trio were swimming in a shrinking pool of open water, unable to migrate to their wintering grounds near Mexico.

Several miles of thick ice separated them from the sea, making their survival impossible without intervention.

The plan to free the whales was ambitious and complicated. Early attempts involved using chainsaws and other tools to carve out pathways through the ice, creating breathing holes for the whales so they could move closer to open water. However, the ice was thick, and the work was slow and dangerous in the extreme Arctic conditions. After word of the rescue efforts spread throughout Alaska, the National Oceanic and Atmospheric Administration (NOAA) sent a team of whale biologists, and the US Department of State requested icebreakers from the Soviet Union to help the cause. In a remarkable demonstration of how environmental concerns could bridge even the most significant geopolitical divides, the Soviets responded by sending two powerful icebreakers.

IÑUPIAT HERITAGE CENTER

WHAT: A museum focused on Iñupiat culture

WHERE: 5421 North Star St., Utqiagvik

COST: Prices vary for adults, children, college students, and locals.

PRO TIP: The Center has a vast exhibit on whales and whaling history in the area.

Photo courtesy of NOAA

While the rescue mission was underway, the whales were given Inuit names: Putu, Siku, and Kanik (meaning Bonnet, Crossbeak, and Bone, respectively).

As time passed, the whales became exhausted, and one of them, Bone, perished. However, with the help of the icebreakers, a path was cleared for the remaining two whales. Though the whales weren't tagged, it is assumed they made their way to freedom.

The event was later adapted into books, documentaries, and even a Hollywood movie titled *Big Miracle* (2012), which dramatized the rescue effort. However, Operation Breakthrough also sparked debates and reflections on the use of resources and the limits of intervention. Critics pointed out that millions of dollars were spent on the rescue, questioning whether it was justified in the grander scheme of environmental conservation. Supporters argued that the event raised global awareness about the fragile Arctic ecosystem and the threats that marine life face due to human activity and climate change.

Though Utqiagvik has a long history of whaling, the Iñupiat don't traditionally harvest gray whales but rather bowhead whales, which have long played a critical role in the community's survival in one of the harshest environments on earth.

BE KIND: REWIND

What does Russell Crowe memorabilia have to do with the last Blockbuster in Alaska?

Late into the 2010s, Blockbuster was a time capsule of the 1990s and early 2000s for many Alaskans, evoking memories of Friday nights spent wandering the aisles, choosing a VHS or DVD, and picking up snacks for a cozy movie night at home. That nostalgia, coupled with slower speeds and more expensive Internet, meant that Alaska remained a stronghold for Blockbuster—a full 11 years after Netflix introduced streaming services and eight years after Blockbuster declared bankruptcy, there were still a handful of outposts of the rental chain in the 49th state.

BLOCKBUSTER

WHAT: The last Blockbuster

WHERE: 211 NE Revere Ave. #3, Bend, OR

COST: Free to visit

PRO TIP: Keep an eye out for the Russell Crowe memorabilia sent from Alaska.

However, in the mid-2010s, the remaining Blockbusters started to shutter. When comedian and host of *Last Week Tonight* John Oliver heard business was faltering, he decided to lend a hand in a truly bizarre way.

Oliver purchased a collection of movie memorabilia from Russell Crowe's divorce auction, including Crowe's jockstrap from *Cinderella Man*, Crowe's director's chair from *American Gangster*, and the vest Crowe wore in *Les Misérables*, among other oddities. Oliver then donated these items to one of the

---

In the years before closure, the last Blockbuster in Anchorage printed and sold T-shirts to fans around the world to help stay afloat.

One of the last Blockbusters in Anchorage, Alaska. Photo courtesy of Doug Moody

remaining Blockbusters in Alaska, hoping they could use the quirky artifacts to draw in curious customers. The Blockbuster on Anchorage's DeBarr Road received and proudly displayed the items. For a brief moment, the store became a media sensation, with visitors coming to see these one-of-a-kind movie relics. However, despite the attention and John Oliver's goodwill, the Anchorage Blockbuster couldn't compete with the unstoppable tide of streaming services and eventually closed, sending Crowe's memorabilia to the last Blockbuster in the United States, located in Bend, Oregon.

A SIDE OF RANCH

Where did the most popular salad dressing in America get its start?

Ranch dressing is one of America's most popular condiments, a staple on salads, chicken wings, and even pizza. But how did this creamy, tangy dressing become a nationwide obsession? It has to do with Alaska and its spirit of making do with what you have.

The story starts in the 1950s when Steve Henson and his wife, Gayle, moved to the Alaskan bush from Nebraska. At the time, Steve was working as a plumbing contractor and experimenting with creating new recipes to feed his crew—a daunting task in an area where food needed to be sent in by bush plane and ingredients needed long shelf lives. One of those recipes called upon buttermilk, mayonnaise, and a blend of dry herbs and spices, which he ladled atop other foodstuffs as a dressing. The creamy concoction was a hit, laying the groundwork for what would become the ranch dressing that's become so ubiquitous across the country today.

In 1954, the Hensons moved to California and purchased a 120-acre guest ranch in Santa Barbara County, which they named Hidden Valley Ranch. The condiment, which they called "ranch dressing" because it was served at the ranch's steakhouse, became so popular with guests that the Hensons began packaging and selling it in dry mix form through the mail. Word spread quickly, and soon, Hidden Valley Ranch was overwhelmed with orders. The Hensons eventually opened a factory to manufacture the dressing and sold it nationwide

---

According to a 2017 study by the Association for Dressings and Sauces, 40 percent of Americans named ranch as their favorite dressing.

Ranch, best served with fried food

before finally selling the company to Clorox in 1972. A decade later, the company devised a way to make the dressing shelf-stable and ready to eat, helping make the dressing a nationwide obsession.

MOOSE'S TOOTH PUB & PIZZERIA

WHAT: A wildly popular pizza restaurant

WHERE: 3300 Old Seward Hwy., Anchorage

COST: Food and drink prices vary.

PRO TIP: This eatery makes its ranch dressing in-house with real buttermilk.

LAUNCHED FROM THE SKY ON THE FOURTH OF JULY

How do you celebrate Independence Day when it's too bright out for fireworks?

In Sutton, Alaska, the Fourth of July means hot dogs, flag-waving, and things going "BOOM." Granted, because the sun doesn't set here during early summer, those explosive noises aren't fireworks but rather a collection of automobiles that are sent screaming off a 300-foot cliff to their doom while crowds cheer.

It's a tradition that started in 2005, and each year, a dozen or so vehicles, ranging from old station wagons to vintage muscle cars long past their prime to the occasional minivan held together by duct tape and hope, get their time to shine (and crash). Before they take flight, the autos are given a paint job and decoration that are equal parts patriotic and bizarre. Flames? Sure. American flags? Absolutely. A random rubber chicken strapped to the roof for good measure? Yeah, why not?

Local businesses and residents sponsor the cars, donating their old beaters or picking up a cheap clunker at auction. There are often last-minute entries, which is why there's no set program for the day, other than the start time.

GLACIER VIEW CAR LAUNCH

WHAT: A one-of-a-kind Fourth of July celebration

WHERE: 34806 W Gamway Dr., Sutton

COST: Entry fee varies for adults and children.

PRO TIP: If you go, bring a chair and cash for food vendors.

Photo courtesy of Claudia Blydenburgh

The vehicles take off from one of two runways. One features a monorail to keep the car on a track, whereas the other is freewheeling. Most of the cars are sent skyward by jamming a simple piece of lumber against the gas pedal and using a ratchet strap to keep the wheel straight. Occasionally, organizers will launch cars off each track, hoping for a mid-air collision (something that's only happened once—it's hard to predict when and how the vehicles will go skyward). One thing is for sure, though: The cars will crash, cartwheel, and ricochet down the bluff before skidding to a stop. And when each vehicle is quieted forever, it gets a standing ovation from the crowd.

If an Independence Day trip to Alaska isn't in the cards, you can catch the highlights online, where the crashes, flips, and occasionally miraculous landings are all captured for posterity.

THE FLOWER MAN LIVES ON

How do you remember a local legend?

Jean Jilwan, called by many as "John The Flower Man," was a staple of downtown Anchorage for nearly 50 years. The friendly, first-generation Lebanese immigrant was known for walking between bars and restaurants each night with a bucket overflowing with multicolored, long-stem roses, which he sold for $5 apiece. During an evening out on the town, it was hard to not run into the enterprising petal peddler.

When Jilwan passed away at 67 years old in September 2020, there was an outpouring of tributes. Myriad people posted on social media about the blossom vendor's kindness and ability to connect with everyone he met, while others penned op-eds for local newspapers and magazines about how their relationship with their spouse started with a rose from Jilwan. Some downtown restaurants "saved" a seat for Jilwan by placing a rose on the bar and bouquets were scattered around downtown Anchorage.

PANCHO'S VILLA

WHAT: A Mexican restaurant where Jean Jilwan's mural is painted

WHERE: 3104 Spenard Rd., Anchorage

COST: Free to visit

PRO TIP: After you visit the mural, head inside for a potent margarita.

Other popular murals in Anchorage include the "Greetings from Alaska" postcard and the Wyland Whaling Wall, at 610 East Fifth Avenue and 320 West Fifth Avenue, respectively.

Petitions were circulated to ask city politicians to find a way to commemorate Jilwan. (One even called for a downtown statue of Captain Cook to be replaced with one of The Flower Man.)

Eventually, a group of local artists (Garrett Perkins, Reed Leslie, Justin Parsons, Rejoy Armamento, and Shara Kay Diamond) hatched a plan to immortalize the downtown legend with a mural with his likeness.

The artists contacted area restaurants to see if they would like some color added to an exterior wall and eventually got permission from Pancho's Villa, a Mexican restaurant that Jilwan popped into at least once (if not two or three times) a night during his almost half-century career as a bloom vendor.

Splashed on a side wall, the piece depicts a black-and-white Jilwan surrounded by a bed of vibrant red, orange, yellow, pink, blue, and purple impressionistic roses.

JUNEAU'S MOST FAMOUS DOG

How did a non-sled dog make history in Juneau?

Set along the waterfront in Juneau, Alaska, is a bronze statue of a dog overlooking the Gastineau Channel. That's Patsy Ann—a local legend whose heartwarming story continues to charm tourists and locals alike.

Despite being deaf from birth, the real-life Patsy Ann was a stray dog with an uncanny ability to "hear" the approaching ships long before they came into sight. Locals swore she could sense when a vessel was drawing near and would eagerly trot down to the docks. She was always first on the scene, barking and wagging her tail as the vessels docked as if she were welcoming them on behalf of the whole town. In fact, in 1934, at 5 years old, Patsy Ann became the "Official Greeter of Juneau," thanks to her joy and dedication to the job. Her ceremony was held just before the timed arrival of the SS *Prince George* to ensure her attendance.

Patsy Ann was known for roaming freely around town and had no problem making herself at home in hotels, restaurants, or even local businesses—never wanting for a scratch or a treat. When the city passed an ordinance requiring all dogs to be licensed, she received a waiver—she belonged to everyone.

PATSY ANN'S MEMORIAL

WHAT: A bronze sculpture memorializing the remarkable life of Juneau's most famous dog

WHERE: 254 Marine Way, Juneau

COST: Free to visit

PRO TIP: You can read the story of Patsy Ann on a nearby sign. Don't forget to give her a pat before you leave.

Photo courtesy of Visit Juneau

After Patsy Ann died in her sleep at the Longshoreman's Union Hall on March 30, 1942, at 14 years old, she was given a burial at sea. Her casket was lowered into the channel near where she had waited for ships. Fifty years later, Patsy Ann returned to her rightful place on the waterfront as the bronze statue. Sculpted by artist Anna Burke Harris, the statue captures Patsy Ann's watchful stance as she gazes out toward the sea. It's as if she's still keeping an eye on things, ready to welcome the next ship with her timeless warmth.

The artist who made the Patsy Ann statue included clippings of dog hair from all over the world in the casting to symbolically unite the spirits of dogs everywhere.

A REMOTE HOMESTEAD

If you could claim any five acres of Alaska, where would you choose?

There are few places with a more spectacular view—or are more remote—than the Don Sheldon Mountain House. Perched on an ice-covered outcrop overlooking Ruth Glacier and just 10 miles from the summit of North America's tallest mountain, Denali, the only way to get to the cabin is by helicopter . . . or a very long hike.

It was built by and named after Don Sheldon, a legendary Alaskan bush pilot. His ability to navigate the complex topography of the Alaska Range made him a sought-after airman, especially for rescue missions—it was he who pioneered glacier landings on Denali. He was also integral to many scientific expeditions, flying geologists, cartographers, and researchers into otherwise inaccessible areas, helping to advance understanding of the Alaskan wilderness.

Before Denali National Park and Preserve expanded to include the peak, Sheldon acquired five acres of land in the 1950s

Adventurers hike up to the Mountain House.

Photos courtesy of Sheldon Chalet

SHELDON CHALET

WHAT: The most remote hotel in the world

WHERE: 10 miles from the summit of Denali

COST: Varies

PRO TIP: Visit in the winter and you might see the northern lights.

as part of the Homestead Act. In 1966, he flew up materials to build a 200-square-foot hexagonal cabin, which was intended to provide shelter for climbers and scientists, as well as be a base for Sheldon's own glacier landings.

He didn't want to stop there—he envisioned building a place where people could experience the raw beauty of Denali without sacrificing comfort. However, he tragically died in 1974 after a battle with colon cancer. His dream finally came to life in 2018 when his children, Robert and Kate Sheldon, completed the luxury retreat called Sheldon Chalet. Also hexagonally shaped, the lodge has five opulent bedrooms, each with close-up views of the granite peak. Guests can spend their days snowshoeing across glaciers, spelunking in snow caverns, and learning how to ice climb.

Sheldon's story is also a powerful reminder of the vital role bush pilots play in remote regions like Alaska where they serve as a lifeline, connecting isolated communities, conducting rescues, and supporting scientific research.

ON THE HALF-SHELL

How do you get oysters in a state where they don't naturally grow?

Alaska has long been hyped as a destination for seafood lovers, thanks to the quality and abundance of the salmon, halibut, rockfish, and crab harvested along the state's shores. However, one sea creature has been making a name for itself in recent years: oysters.

Interestingly, oysters don't naturally grow in Alaska. The waters off the coast are just warm enough (and full of more than enough plankton) for the oysters to thrive once in the water, but it's too cold for them to reach sexual maturity, and therefore they can't reproduce.

HUMP ISLAND OYSTER CO.

WHAT: An oyster farm that offers tours and tastings

WHERE: 7180 Revilla Rd,, Ketchikan

COST: Varies

PRO TIP: Also be sure to try their kelp salsa.

Instead, farmers take oyster "seeds" (juvenile bivalves) that are flown in from out of state or born in labs within Alaska and transplant them in suspended nets in the bay, where they continue to grow for several years until they are restaurant-ready.

What makes Alaskan oysters so unique is that they're sweeter (due to the cold growing conditions) and cleaner than

In summer months, when oysters elsewhere in the country are soft and milky, the Alaska bivalves stay crisp and fresh. Because they can't spawn, Alaska oysters are safe to eat year-round (not just months with the letter "r" in them).

oysters found elsewhere in the US (because they're grown off the ocean floor, they don't get sand in them and therefore also never make pearls). The nets also gently toss the oysters, which helps give them deep cups full of plump meat as opposed to long and shallow shells.

Left: *Oysters on the half-shell and ready to eat*

Below: *Oysters just pulled from the ocean*

IT'S HAMMER TIME

Have you ever wondered how many types of hammers exist?

You'll know you've arrived at the Hammer Museum in Haines, Alaska—it's the building with a 20-foot-tall hammer in the front yard.

At any given time, there are more than 2,500 hammers on display (and more than 8,000 in storage) at this unique museum. Some of these even date back to the ancient Romans. However, not all of the instruments are meant for driving nails or breaking objects. Among the hardware, there are wooden hammers used for cracking lobster claws, gavels from fraternal organizations, and mini-mallets used in 1930s cocktail clubs to tap on glassware as a polite form of applause. There are also exhibits on the myriad occupations that have used hammers, from builders and miners to musicians and bookbinders, as well as the patents for several thousand hammers that explain how each inventor planned for their tool to be used.

The proprietor, Dave Pahl, opened the ode to one of mankind's first tools in 2002—he needed somewhere to display his vast collection after he ran out of wall space in his home. While digging a basement that would help transform a run-down building on Main Street into a functioning museum, Pahl found a Tlingit warrior pick in

THE HAMMER MUSEUM

WHAT: A museum dedicated to hammers

WHERE: 108 Main St., Haines

COST: Price varies for adults, as well as active military, veterans, and their spouses. Free for children 12 and under.

PRO TIP: If you visit outside of the summer tourist season, call ahead.

Photos courtesy of Visit Haines

the dirt, which he took as a sign he'd chosen the right spot to set up shop.

If you ask, he can tell you almost anything you'd care to know about hammers. He knows so much about the instrument that the Smithsonian Institution has previously asked him to help identify tools in their collection, and the History Channel has asked for advice on which hammers to use for accurate reenactments.

In 2016, the museum was featured on *Jeopardy!* under the category "Offbeat Museums." The clue: "Haines, Alaska's museum of this tool features exhibits on handle making and '5 ways not to hit your fingers.'"

EIGHT GOLD STARS IN A BLUE SKY

Who designed Alaska's state flag?

The story of Alaska's state flag began in 1927 when the then territory decided it needed an official flag. The hope was that a banner of its own would help with its bid for statehood.

To find the would-be symbol of the territory, the American Legion, a veterans' organization, sponsored a design contest open to all Alaskan children from grades 7 to 12, offering a gold watch and a $1,000 scholarship as the prize for the winning proposal.

Out of more than 700 entries, the unanimous first-place choice came from a 13-year-old boy named Benny Benson. Born in Chignik, a small fishing village on the Alaska Peninsula, Benny was an orphan of Aleut, Russian, and Swedish descent, living at the Jesse Lee Home for Children in Seward, Alaska.

Benny's flag design featured eight gold stars set against a dark blue background. Seven of the stars form the

BENNY BENSON MEMORIAL PARK

WHAT: A park with a walking trail along a lake

WHERE: Dairy Hill Ln., Seward

COST: Free to visit

PRO TIP: Look for the mosaic memorial commemorating Benny Benson at the park's entrance.

The original flag—made of blue silk and handsewn gold stars—and the watch Benny donated in 1963 are all housed at the Alaska State Museum.

constellation Ursa Major, otherwise known as the Big Dipper, which symbolizes the Great Bear, an emblem of strength. The eighth star represents the North Star, a nod to Alaska's northernmost position in the United States. The blue background represents the sky and the forget-me-not, a dainty blue flower native to Alaska.

The territorial legislature officially adopted Benson's flag design on May 2, 1927. And when Alaska joined the Union on January 3, 1959, it became the flag of the State of Alaska.

SLEEPING LADY

How long would you wait for the love of your life?

Officially, the roughly 4,400-foot-tall mountain that dominates the skyline across the Cook Inlet from Anchorage is known as Mount Susitna. Located approximately 33 miles northwest of Anchorage, on the western bank of the lower Susitna River, the mountain is perhaps better known locally as "The Sleeping Lady" because it looks like the silhouette of a recumbent woman.

The moniker is derived from an Indigenous folktale, which says the mountain was once a beautiful young woman named Susitna, who came from an ancient tribe of giants many millennia ago. Susitna was engaged to Nekatla, a brave warrior who had to leave on the eve of their wedding to try to convince another tribe threatening war to live in peace and harmony. Before departing, Nekatla told Susitna to wait for him at their favorite plateau. For days, she waited, occupying her time picking berries and weaving baskets. Eventually, she grew weary and lay down to rest before falling into a deep sleep.

When news later reached the tribe that Nekatla and the other warriors who had traveled with him had been captured or struck down in a fierce battle, the other villagers couldn't bear to wake Susitna up. Instead, they covered her in a blanket of grass and wildflowers and let her slumber, forever frozen in time, waiting for her betrothed to return. Some versions of the story say Susitna will awaken when the world knows peace.

Long shared as a folk legend, versions of the tale have since become immortalized in print. In 1994, author Ann

---

Other good viewing points of Sleeping Lady include the Tony Knowles Coastal Trail and along the Parks Highway in the Matanuska-Susitna Valley.

49TH STATE BREWING COMPANY

WHAT: A brewery with excellent views of Mount Susitna

WHERE: 717 W 3rd Ave., Anchorage

COST: Varies

PRO TIP: Head to the patio or roof for the best views.

Dixon adapted the story into a children's picture book titled *The Sleeping Lady*. Her retelling accounts for both the origin of the state's first snowfall and how Mount Susitna came to be. Similarly, in *A Dena'ina Legacy*, Peter Kalifornsky, an Indigenous writer and ethnographer, added that Susitna's relatives also lay down and became what are now known as Mount Redoubt, Mount Iliamna, and Denali.

COWABUNGA, DUDE

What is a bore tide and how do you see it in Alaska?

It's hard not to talk about Alaska without using superlatives. It has the tallest mountain in North America, the largest glacial system in the United States, and the most coastline of any state, just to name a few. It also has one of the largest bore tides in the world.

BELUGA POINT

WHAT: A pull-off from the Seward Highway that provides a wide-open view of the Arm as the wave approaches

WHERE: Mile 110, Seward Hwy., Anchorage

COST: Free

PRO TIP: The best viewing times are typically during the days following a full or new moon, when the tidal range is at its highest.

Twice a day, a single monstrous wave (reaching heights up to 10 feet tall and barreling along as fast as 15 miles per hour) surges through the entire 50-mile length of the narrow moutain-and-highway-lined inlet known as Turnagain Arm.

Basically, a bore tide is what happens when there's a massive difference of depth (about 40 feet in this case) between the water level at low tide and high tide. When the incoming high tide hits the shallower waters of the Turnagain Arm, it has nowhere to go but forward, creating a dramatic surge of water. While bore tides happen worldwide, Turnagain Arm is one of the few where the phenomenon can be observed regularly—this long, narrow, and shallow body of water is uniquely suited to produce bore tides due to its funnel-like shape, which amplifies the incoming tide.

Local surfers like to try to catch the wave—if they make it, they can ride it for roughly 50 miles. There are many pull-out points along the Seward Highway to watch the wave or take pictures of the impossibly scenic area, with some of the most

Photo courtesy of Greatland Adventures

popular being Beluga Point and Bird Ridge. Hope, a town across the Turnagain Arm, is a good spot as well. You're also more likely to see harbor seals and beluga whales after the bore tide comes in—they like to ride the wave, too.

While the bore tide is mesmerizing, it also poses risks. The mudflats along the Turnagain Arm are notoriously dangerous, with quicksand-like conditions that can trap unsuspecting visitors. It is essential to observe safety guidelines, stay on solid ground, and exercise caution when near the water's edge.

THE BAWDY PAST OF CREEK STREET

How did one of Ketchikan's most picturesque tourist districts get its start?

When cruise ships are in port, you can expect the historic boardwalk above Ketchikan Creek to be busy—not only does it offer an incredible viewing point for watching salmon charge upstream to lay their eggs, but it's also lined with charming historic buildings that now house art galleries, gift shops, and restaurants. Don't let the colorful facades fool you—the more than 120-year-old walkway has a bawdy history.

Built in 1903, the street's over-water location was a practical solution to the limited amount of flat land in Ketchikan, which is surrounded by steep hills and dense forest. Creek Street quickly became the town's entertainment hub, where men working in fishing and logging could find the nightly diversions of gambling, bootleg liquor, and the company of women.

During Prohibition, Creek Street thrived as a center for speakeasies. Cleverly designed escape routes and trapdoors allowed patrons to board well-concealed rowboats or dip out onto Married Man's Trail to evade the law during sudden raids. Liquor would be smuggled in from Canada via "hooch runs," and secret stashes were often hidden under the very boardwalks that now support the bustling tourist shops and galleries.

When the city outlawed prostitution in 1954, Creek Street became a mixed residential and commercial area, but you can still read the tales of Creek Street's notorious past on plaques along the boardwalk.

Post-Prohibition, Creek Street's most infamous aspect remained its role as Ketchikan's red-light district. At its height, it supported 30 brothels and was known as the only place in Alaska where "the fishermen and the fish went upstream to spawn." From the early 1900s until the 1950s, the street was home to a series of bordellos that catered to the town's transient male workforce. The most famous of these was Dolly's House, operated by Dolly Arthur, a madam who lived and worked on Creek Street for over 30 years.

DOLLY'S HOUSE MUSEUM

WHAT: The only Creek Street "den of iniquity" that still stands (however, it's now a museum)

WHERE: 24 Creek St., Ketchikan

COST: Fee for admission

PRO TIP: Look for the secret closet in Dolly's bedroom—it's where she stashed contraband liquor during Prohibition.

Creek Street in Ketchikan is built on stilts. Photo courtesy of Visit Ketchikan

ALL ABOARD AND GOING NOWHERE

Where will the aging train line from Nome take you?

Stretching 35 miles into the desolate horizon from Nome is a steel railway that terminates at a trio of ghostly locomotives sinking into the tundra. It's the Last Train to Nowhere.

In the wake of the gold rush, entrepreneurs sought to carve out their fortunes in the frozen north. One such vision was the creation of a railway that would connect the remote seaside community of Nome to the rich gold fields that had sprung up in the state's vast interior. Called the Nome-Arctic Railway, it was an ambitious project that promised to bring prosperity and connection to one of the most isolated regions in the world.

Construction began in 1903 after three 1880s-era locomotives (retired from the New York Elevated rail system), a clutch of boxcars and flat cars, and more than 50 miles of track had been shipped to Nome by boat. However, the harsh realities of the

THE LAST TRAIN TO NOWHERE

WHAT: The final resting spot for some more than 100-year-old trains

WHERE: Nome

COST: Free

PRO TIP: Follow the Nome-Council Road northeast from Nome until you cross the Bonanza Bridge—the trains are just off the side of the road.

Today there are viewing platforms and educational signs that share the story of the Last Train to Nowhere.

Photo courtesy of Shauntel Bruner Alvanna

Alaskan wilderness soon became apparent. Permafrost, extreme weather, and logistical challenges plagued the project from the start. Despite the builders' best efforts, the railway never reached its intended destination. Within just a few years, the project was abandoned near Solomon, leaving behind a partially completed track and a handful of rusting steam locomotives—the last echoes of a dream long abandoned.

SPINNING A YARN

What exactly is qiviut, and why is it so special?

When it comes to luxurious fibers, most people think of cashmere, silk, or merino wool. However, there is a rare, almost mythical material that stands in a league of its own: qiviut. Pronounced "kiv-ee-oot," it is softer than cashmere and warmer than wool, making it a highly coveted natural fiber, though many have never heard of it.

Qiviut belongs to the musk ox, a large, shaggy mammal native to the Arctic tundra. For millennia, musk oxen have roamed the frozen landscapes of North America, surviving in some of the harshest climates on earth. To endure these extreme conditions, musk oxen have evolved to develop an extraordinary double-layered coat. The outer layer consists of long, coarse guard hairs that protect them from wind and moisture. The downy inner layer, the qiviut, helps insulate the animals and keep them warm in temperatures as low as minus 40 degrees Fahrenheit.

Musk oxen naturally shed their undercoats each spring as temperatures rise. This qiviut is then collected by hand, traditionally by gathering the tumbleweed-like tufts left behind on the tundra. After harvesting, the raw fiber is meticulously cleaned and spun into yarn. The end product is an incredibly soft, cloud-like yarn that is both luxurious and practical. A single skein of qiviut yarn can cost hundreds of dollars, and

---

Musk oxen are not widely domesticated, and their natural habitats are remote and challenging to access, which contributes to the high cost of the fibers. Additionally, each musk ox produces only a small amount of qiviut each year—typically around 4 to 7 pounds.

A baby musk ox resting at the Musk Ox Farm.

THE MUSK OX FARM

WHAT: A nonprofit farm featuring musk oxen

WHERE: 12850 E Archie Rd., Palmer

COST: Prices vary for adults and children.

PRO TIP: Be sure to check out the gift shop—there's typically qiviut sweaters and yarn on sale.

garments made from the fiber are considered heirloom pieces, often passed down through generations.

For those interested in seeing where qiviut comes from and learning more about these Arctic animals, the Musk Ox Farm in Palmer, Alaska, is a must-visit destination. This unique farm is dedicated to the domestication and preservation of the musk ox, with a focus on sustainable agriculture and cultural heritage.

AN UNLIKELY OUTPOST

Where is the only place you can legally enter the US by land without reporting to a border official?

Hyder, a tiny settlement tucked away on the edge of the Tongass National Forest, is the southernmost city in Alaska reachable by car. However, you can't drive to Hyder from any other city in Alaska.

The community is located at the head of Portland Canal, a fjord that forms part of the US–Canada border. Due to unique geographical barriers, the only way to get to Hyder is by first visiting Stewart, a town of roughly 500 people just across the border in British Columbia. From there, it's only a short drive across the international boundary to Hyder.

There is no US Customs checkpoint entering Hyder from Canada, though you must report to the Canada Border Services Agency on the way back. Often, the border seems more like a formality than a true divide. The reality is that Hyder residents rely on Stewart for everyday services—things like groceries and fuel come through the Canadian town and local kids are sent across the border for school. And though Alaskans love to say the area code for the entire state is 907, that's not exactly true. In Hyder, the community uses British Columbia's 250 area code instead, even though it's an entirely different nation.

The town has a decidedly blended nature. Both American and Canadian holidays are observed there, and though it's in the United States, shops accept Canadian currency alongside

---

In downtown Stewart, the Stewart Museum, run by the local historical society, shares how Hyder was started as a mining town after gold and silver were found in the area in the late 1890s.

dollars (everywhere except the US Post Office). Similarly, although the community is technically in the Alaska Time Zone, clocks are set to British Columbia's Pacific Time.

Today, fewer than 50 residents live in Hyder. After the nearby mines ran dry, the population dwindled. Over time, the former boom town adopted the moniker "The Friendliest Ghost Town in Alaska." For travelers, the town's biggest draws are some gold rush–era saloons and the Fish Creek Wildlife Observation Site, where from mid-July to September visitors can watch brown and black bears feast on salmon from elevated boardwalks.

GLACIER INN

WHAT: A hotel and bar

WHERE: International St., Hyder

COST: Varies

PRO TIP: Visitors come here to get "Hyderized." It involves downing a shot of 150-proof grain alcohol. Once completed, you'll receive a certificate that declares you've officially been initiated into the community.

Top: *Photo courtesy of Stewart Tourism*

Bottom: *Photo courtesy of Caroline Stewart*

HOOT, HOWL, BUGLE, AND ROAR

What does it take to reintroduce animals into the wild?

One bucket list item for Alaska visitors is often to see moose and bears, though considering they're wild animals, that's usually easier said than done. However, visiting the Alaska Wildlife Conservation Center (AWCC) is one way to stack the deck. Nestled in the staggeringly beautiful Portage Valley and surrounded by the majestic Chugach Mountains, this 200-acre sanctuary offers visitors a unique opportunity to experience Alaska's wildlife up close.

The center is home to various species, including bears, moose, elk, and musk oxen. Each of these animals has a story, often involving rescue and rehabilitation, like Hugo, a grizzly bear who was brought to AWCC for treatment and a permanent home after she was found as a cub near Kotzebue with hundreds of porcupine quills in her paws.

ALASKA WILDLIFE CONSERVATION CENTER

WHAT: A nonprofit organization dedicated to animal research and care

WHERE: 43520 Seward Hwy., Girdwood

COST: Prices vary for adults and children.

PRO TIP: On certain days during the summer, guests can hand-feed AWCC's moose for an additional fee. The center is open to the public for private tours by request or during events.

One of the highlights of the AWCC experience is the chance to see wood bison. Once considered extinct, these majestic creatures were rediscovered in a remote area of Canada in the 1950s. Recognizing the ecological significance of the species, the AWCC partnered with state and federal agencies to reintroduce wood bison to the wild in Alaska. In the early

Kuma the black bear at the Alaska Wildlife Conservation Center. Photo courtesy of Bill Szepanski/Alaska Wildlife Conservation Center

2000s, a small herd was brought to the center, where they were carefully bred and cared for with the goal of reintroducing them to their natural habitat.

The program faced numerous challenges, including ensuring the bison could adapt to the wild after generations in captivity. However, in 2015, after years of meticulous planning and preparation, the AWCC successfully released the first group of wood bison into the wild in the Innoko River region. This reintroduction marked the first time in over a century that wood bison roamed the Alaskan wilderness. Today, the herd continues to grow and thrive, and more wood bison are periodically released into the wild.

Scenes of *Into the Wild* were filmed at the AWCC, including one where the protagonist butchers a moose. In reality, AWCC's resident moose weren't hurt in the making of the movie—a roadkill moose was used.

WILDERNESS WOMAN

Do you have what it takes to be a single woman in rural Alaska?

Living in a dry cabin in the Alaska wilderness takes a certain kind of person. But beyond the grit and mental fortitude to do battle with Jack Frost each winter, they need a particular skill set. And one yearly contest sets out to prove which women are best suited for the lifestyle.

Started in 1986, the Wilderness Woman competition was conceived as a tongue-in-cheek response to the shortage of single women in Talkeetna. Each year in early December, 50 women from across Alaska compete in a series of rigorous and often humorous challenges designed to showcase the skills necessary for surviving in the Bush. The only barriers for entry are they need to be single (in this case, meaning not married or engaged) and they need to be at least 21 years old.

The competition kicks off with (often costumed) contenders racing down Main Street with two empty five-gallon water buckets, exchanging them for full ones and getting back across the finish line without spilling. It's a game meant to replicate the daily chore of fetching water for those who live in dry cabins.

The five fastest times move on to the next rounds, which involve tasks like running in snowshoes, splitting and hauling wood on a snow machine (snowmobile to Lower 48ers), catching fish, shooting a "ptarmigan" (usually a balloon) and

---

The Wilderness Woman contest is always the same day as the Bachelor Ball at the Sheldon Community Arts Hangar, where local men are auctioned off (for a drink and a dance), with the proceeds going toward women and children in crisis.

Photo courtesy of the Talkeetna Bachelor Society

a "moose" (a costumed man), and delivering a sandwich (which they make themselves) and beer to a bachelor (often wearing a trash bag poncho, as there are no rules about doing so gently) in a lounge chair. In the past, the winner has received a plaque and a fur hat.

WILDERNESS WOMAN COMPETITION

WHAT: A contest that sees single women proving their ability to perform skills necessary for living in rural Alaska

WHERE: Main St., Talkeetna

COST: Free

PRO TIP: Sign-ups for the contest open online a month beforehand; however it's also possible to sign up the day of the competition at the Fairview Inn.

A CHOCOLATE CASCADE

What does 3,400 pounds of melted chocolate look like?

The Guinness World Records recognizes a slew of chocolate-centered titles, ranging from the largest chocolate bar by area (1,531.9 square feet) to the longest chocolate sculpture (a 111-foot, 8-inch train). Though it doesn't currently recognize the world's tallest chocolate waterfall, if it did, it would be the 20-foot-tall, Willy Wonka–esque marvel at Alaska Wild Berry Products.

This mesmerizing installation, built by Homer artist Mike Sirl in the early '90s, features over 3,400 pounds of rich, liquid chocolate that continuously cascades down a series of copper candy kettles into a swirling pool of velvety cocoa, creating a visual and aromatic experience that's as captivating as it is mouthwatering.

The molten treat is donated by two of the biggest names in chocolate: Nestlé and Guittard. And though it may be tempting to sample from the giant fondue fountain (or pull an Augustus Gloop and go for a swim), it's important to note that the molten chocolate isn't for eating.

While the chocolate waterfall is the star attraction, Alaska Wild Berry Products offers much more to explore. The store is a paradise for food lovers, with shelves stocked full of handcrafted chocolates, wild berry jams, jellies, syrups, and

ALASKA WILD BERRY PRODUCTS

WHAT: A chocolate shop featuring a world-record chocolate waterfall

WHERE: 5225 Juneau St., Anchorage

COST: Free to visit

PRO TIP: The store also features a gift shop filled with Alaskan souvenirs, from artisanal crafts to local artwork, making it a perfect stop for those looking to bring home a piece of Alaska.

Photo courtesy of Alaska Wild Berry Products

other treats made from Alaskan ingredients. Visitors can sample a wide variety of confections, watch candy-making demonstrations, and learn about the importance of Alaska's wild berries.

In 2023, Alaska Wild Berry Products's waterfall was named the largest on earth by the World Record Academy.

BUNKING DOWN IN HISTORY

What does it take to save a piece of history?

In the early 1900s, more than 3,000 roadhouses were scattered along Alaska's road, trail, and river systems to cater to the miners, trappers, and other fortune-seekers streaming into the territory. The roadhouses were usually set every 10 or 12 miles apart (thought to be the distance someone could walk with all their belongings on their back in a single day), and, because they were the only business around, they were a hybrid of a lodge, restaurant, saloon, post office, store, community center, and whatever else travelers needed them to be. And in the winter, they were a particularly important reprieve from the elements.

However, with the expansion of the railway system and, later, the advent of better roads and cars, which allowed people to travel great distances much more quickly, roadhouses became obsolete. And over the years, their fates were sealed by earthquakes, fires, and abandonment—today there are only about two dozen roadhouses left in Alaska.

A few, like the Talkeetna Roadhouse in Talkeetna and Meiers Lake Roadhouse in Gakona, still serve their communities in the same way as they always have. Others, like Sullivan Roadhouse in Delta Junction and Rika's Roadhouse near Big Delta, have been made into museums and art galleries. (Fox Roadhouse, just north of Fairbanks, became part of Silver Gulch Brewery.)

Most of the roadhouses that have survived into the new millennium are on major thoroughfares like the Richardson Highway, the Glenn Highway, and the Park Highway.

Talkeetna Roadhouse, one of the last roadhouses in Alaska

While most roadhouses were lost, some conservationists are trying to revive the ones that didn't make it through Alaska's settler era, like the dilapidated Black Rapids Roadhouse near Delta Junction. If successful, they'll help keep some of Alaska's adventurous spirit alive for generations to come.

THE LODGE AT BLACK RAPIDS

WHAT: An adventure lodge on the same property as the historic Black Rapids Roadhouse (which they're working on restoring)

WHERE: Mile 227.4, Richardson Hwy., 38 miles south of Delta Junction

COST: Free to visit, though the price to stay overnight varies

PRO TIP: The roadhouse was once owned by Frank Glaser, an Alaskan known for using wolf puppies for dog sledding and who fought off grizzlies.

ICE, ICE BABY

What is the largest glacier in North America?

Whether you're standing at the foot of a massive ice wall, cruising through waterways dotted with icebergs, or soaring above the glaciers in a small plane, the experience of seeing a glacier, with its otherworldly blue hues and Seussically strange shapes, is sure to leave you with a deep appreciation for the raw beauty of nature. And there's arguably no better place to witness these massive, dynamic, ever-changing rivers of ice than in Alaska, where there are more active glaciers than anywhere else in the inhabited world.

Glaciers cover more than five percent of Alaska—that's more than 33,000 square miles, an area roughly the size of

South Carolina. In fact, there are over 100,000 glaciers within the state, only a third of which have official names, even though some have been around for more than 30,000 years. They range from tiny cirque glaciers that form in a bowl-shaped depression on the side of a mountain to sprawling valley glaciers.

The largest is Bering Glacier, near Cordova in the state's southeast. Combined with the ice fields that feed into it, it's 126 miles long and covers an area of more than 1,900 square miles, making it the biggest on the continent.

Some—like Ruth Glacier, the top of which is just three vertical miles from the summit of Denali—are a long trek or an expensive charter plane to get to. Similarly, tidewater glaciers (meaning the floe terminates in the ocean), such as Surprise Glacier, Margerie Glacier, and Columbia Glacier, require a boat to see. Still, there are others, like Matanuska Glacier, Portage Glacier, Exit Glacier, and Root Glacier, that you can drive right up to or do a quick hike to reach.

MENDENHALL GLACIER VISITOR CENTER

WHAT: The visitor center for the 13-mile-long, half-mile-wide Mendenhall Glacier

WHERE: 8150 Mendenhall Loop Rd., Juneau

COST: Fee for admission

PRO TIP: To really appreciate the floe, consider hiring a glacier-trekking guide and spend the afternoon on the ice.

Alaska's glaciers are not just a stunning natural attraction—they are also at the forefront of climate change. Many of them are retreating at an unprecedented rate, a stark reminder of the environmental changes affecting the planet.

BLUE BABE

Would you eat 36,000-year-old game meat?

At the University of Alaska Museum of the North, it's possible to see a creature that once roamed Alaska alongside woolly mammoths and saber-toothed cats.

It's a steppe bison that for over 36,000 years was buried deep beneath the icy permafrost, mummifying it in near-perfect condition, before being unearthed in 1979 by a group of gold miners near Fairbanks. It was named "Blue Babe" due to the bluish hue of its preserved hide, resulting from the chemical reaction between the iron in the animal's blood and the surrounding soil (it's also a tongue-in-cheek reference to Paul Bunyan's giant blue ox).

Given the claw and tooth marks on Blue Babe's rear, scientists determined that Blue Babe likely died after a run-in with an Ice Age American lion. Still, the remarkable state of Blue Babe's preservation has allowed researchers to conduct detailed studies on the bison's diet, habitat, and environmental conditions of the time. By analyzing the contents of Blue Babe's stomach, scientists have been able to reconstruct its last meal,

UNIVERSITY OF ALASKA MUSEUM OF THE NORTH

WHAT: A world-renowned cultural and historical museum that's home to Blue Babe

WHERE: 1962 Yukon Dr., Fairbanks

COST: Entry fee; free for children ages 5 and under

PRO TIP: Come for Blue Babe, stay for the exhibits on Indigenous cultures, Alaska wildlife, and the forces that shaped the landscapes of the region.

Blue Babe is the only known Pleistocene bison to have been recovered from permafrost.

Top: *Photo courtesy of Sherman Hogie/Explore Fairbanks*

Bottom: *Photo courtesy of Museum of the North*

providing clues about the vegetation that existed in Alaska during the Pleistocene era.

A few years after the bison came to the Museum of the North, Eirik Granqvist, a Finnish taxidermist, came and got the Blue Babe exhibition ready, removing and treating the animal's skin and mounting it on a plaster replica. After the work was done, Dale Guthrie, the paleontologist overseeing Blue Babe, hosted a dinner party where eight guests dined on a stew made of stock, vegetables, and meat from the bison's neck. In the *Food History Almanac*, Guthrie wrote, "When it thawed, it gave off an unmistakable beef aroma, not unpleasantly mixed with a faint smell of the earth in which it was found, with a touch of mushroom."

HERE COMES THE (MIDNIGHT) SUN

What would you do with a full day of sunlight?

POINT BARROW

WHAT: The northernmost point in the United States

WHERE: Utqiagvik

COST: Free to visit

PRO TIP: The Iñupiat name for Point Barrow is Nuwak or Nuvuk, which means "point of land." It's an excellent Midnight Sun viewing spot.

Utqiagvik (formerly known as Barrow), the northernmost city in the United States, has interesting bragging rights: It has both the longest and shortest day of the year. Because of the earth's tilt, when the sun rises in early May, it doesn't set again for nearly three months (on the other end of the spectrum, when it sets in mid-November, locals don't see the sun again for almost two months).

The Midnight Sun is most famously seen above the Arctic Circle, though all of Alaska experiences long summer days. Anchorage, for instance, sees

three hours and 42 minutes of daylight on the winter solstice and 19 hours and 22 minutes on the summer solstice.

It's a beautiful time to be in the state—because the sun hangs so low on the horizon, it bathes the land in a soft rose-gold light, and sunsets last for hours.

All that extra light extends your exploration window, so it's not uncommon to see people enjoying time outdoors late into the night. And in June, around the summer solstice (June 20th or 21st, depending on the year), some of the larger cities, like Anchorage and Nome, host festivals featuring live music, food vendors, and family-friendly activities—all while the sky remains brightly lit well into the early hours of the morning. Fairbanks's festival also features a Midnight Sun baseball game, which starts at 10 p.m. and never requires artificial light, even if they go into extra innings.

If you visit Alaska during the summer months, it's a good idea to come with eye masks and to opt for hotels with blackout curtains—that is, if you want to sleep.

Two a.m. in the land of the Midnight Sun

ON THE ROCKS

How do you construct a bar entirely made of ice?

Located about 60 miles northeast of Fairbanks, the Chena Hot Springs are a geothermal wonder. For more than a century, their steaming mineral-rich waters have soothed the ailments of visitors, from gold miners to remote workers. However, it's far from the only reason to visit the resort of the same name—nor the only thing there that will erase your problems (at least temporarily).

The Chena Hot Springs Resort is also home to the world-famous Aurora Ice Museum, where visitors ogle over-the-top ice sculptures and sip cocktails from frozen glasses in sub-zero surroundings all year long.

AURORA ICE MUSEUM

WHAT: The world's largest year-round ice museum and bar

WHERE: 17600 Chena Hot Springs Rd., Fairbanks

COST: Varies for adults and children

PRO TIP: The entire space is kept at a brisk 25 degrees Fahrenheit, so be sure to bundle up.

Photo courtesy of Sherman Hogue/Explore Fairbanks

Completed in 2005, the museum was constructed from more than 1,000 tons of ice and snow. The building itself is the brainchild of renowned ice carver Steve Brice and his wife, Heather, who have spent years perfecting the art form. Some of the pieces, such as the ice turret and the jousting knight scene, have been there since the beginning, while most of the others are rotated out every year to keep the experience fresh and mesmerizing for returning guests.

The bar is open only during tours, which run every other hour starting at 11 a.m. After the tour ends, guests are cut loose to explore, with most people finishing the experience by pulling up a caribou-hide-covered ice stool at the bar and sipping on the signature appletini.

The lighting in the Aurora Ice Museum shifts between shades of green, pink, and blue—it's supposed to mimic the northern lights.

WORLD-TRAVELING TOTEMS

How did a totem pole from southeast Alaska end up in Indianapolis?

It was the fall of 1903, and then-governor John Brady had big plans for some Haida and Tlingit totem poles. Eventually, the totems would be installed in a brand-new park in Sitka, preserved where anyone who wished could see them. But first, they had to take a trip to St. Louis.

> **SITKA NATIONAL HISTORICAL PARK**
>
> **WHAT:** A 113-acre coastal rainforest park that is home to the 1904 World's Fair totem poles
>
> **WHERE:** 103 Monastery St., Sitka
>
> **COST:** Free to visit
>
> **PRO TIP:** Sitka's master carvers often work on new totems in a pavilion within the park and are happy to answer questions about their pieces.

The World's Fair was slated to kick off the following year, and Brady, motivated by a bid for statehood, wanted the Alaska Pavilion to really stand out from the others. He figured a clutch of authentic, 30-foot-tall totem poles would create buzz.

So he rounded up 15 totem poles that had been donated by chiefs of coastal island villages all over southeast Alaska and had them shipped to Missouri. Fourteen totems were erected around two replicas of Indigenous dwellings—the 15th was installed at a separate exhibit meant to look like a Klondike mining camp.

When the fair wrapped, 13 poles were shipped back to Alaska—Brady decided to sell the other two, as they weren't in good enough condition to make the return journey. One ended up at the Milwaukee Public Museum, where it remains today.

Right: *One of the many totem poles in Sitka Historical Park. Photo courtesy of Visit Sitka.* Left: *Photo courtesy of National Park Service*

However, for many years historians weren't sure what happened to the other—the lone pole from the Klondike exhibit.

It wasn't until the '90s that the fate of the pole was unearthed. It turned out Brady had sold the piece to Russell E. Gardner, the founder of Banner Buggy Company (which made horse-drawn carriages and later automobile bodies), who then turned around and gave it to a prominent industrialist named David M. Parry, who had it raised on his estate in Indianapolis. It stayed there until 1939, when it fell during a storm due to rot.

The lost pole bore the likeness of a long-snouted sea monster, a bear, and a man—it told the story of a man who was in conflict with his mother-in-law.

THE ONLY WAY OUT IS THROUGH IT

How do cars and trains get through a single-lane tunnel?

Sandwiched between the waters of the Passage Canal and the 3,500-foot peaks of the Chugach Mountain Range, Whittier isn't an easy place to visit. To get there, you'll need to either arrive by boat or drive through the Anton Anderson Memorial Tunnel.

Often simply called the Whittier Tunnel, this 2.5-mile-long passageway was constructed during World War II to serve as a military supply route to the strategically important Whittier harbor.

Though its original use was for rail traffic alone, in 2000 it was adapted for dual use, allowing vehicles to traverse this underground passageway. The single-lane tunnel is shared between cars and trains, meaning that traffic in each direction takes turns passing through. Coordinated by a timed schedule, this alternating flow means that drivers queue up on the approach road and wait for the green light that signals their turn to enter the mountain. The walls are rough-hewn and rugged,

Photo courtesy of Whittier Chamber of Commerce

Whittier landscape

ANTON ANDERSON MEMORIAL TUNNEL

WHAT: A 2.5-mile, single-lane mountain tunnel that connects Whittier and Girdwood

WHERE: Portage Glacier Rd., Girdwood

COST: Fee for round-trip ticket

PRO TIP: Cars to Whittier leave on the half hour; cars from Whittier leave on the hour.

and at its widest, the tunnel is just over 18 feet, though the driving surface is just 7.5 feet wide, making it a snug passage for modern vehicles. For that reason, the speed limit is just 25 miles per hour.

Still, as the longest combined vehicle-railroad tunnel in North America, it is an engineering marvel that offers travelers more than just a practical route—it's a gateway to adventure, nature, and history. As you exit the tunnel into the port town of Whittier, you're greeted by a sweeping panorama of the Prince William Sound and the towering trees of the Chugach National Forest.

Whittier is a hub for fishing and hiking, but for many travelers, its deep-water port is the jumping-off point for cruises, sea kayaking, or wildlife tours in the Sound.

BEWARE THE CRAB

Did an Alaska hotel kill a US president?

Shortly after the Fairview Inn was completed in 1923, it hosted arguably its most famous guest: President Warren G. Harding. Harding was on his Voyage of Understanding tour and was in Alaska to promote the newly completed Alaska Railroad, making him the first sitting president to visit the territory. While his visit to the Fairview Inn was brief, it may have influenced the rest of his life.

The president died less than a week later, and since then, there's been a persistent rumor that the 29th commander in chief was felled by ptomaine poisoning from the Fairview's crab leg special. Other tales claimed a local man gave him toxin-laced tobacco or that his wife slipped something noxious into his meal in Alaska as an act of retaliation for his philandering. Various other conspiracy theories that didn't involve Harding's time in Alaska followed his death, ranging from murder by political opponents to suicide so that he wouldn't have to deal with the embarrassment of a possible impeachment from his many scandals. The actual cause of death could have been determined with an autopsy; however, the president's widow refused to authorize one, which only added to the drama surrounding his demise.

FAIRVIEW INN

WHAT: A historic hotel and saloon that may or may not have had a hand in President Harding's death

WHERE: 101 N Main St., Talkeetna

COST: Free to visit; price of meals, drinks, and accommodation varies.

PRO TIP: In the summer, stop by for drinks in the beer garden.

Whether the lunchtime special actually 86'd the president or not, we'll never know. But the historic hotel has leaned into

Photos courtesy of Tom Bol Photography/ Mat-Su CVB

the idea that its cooking played a role. While no longer on the menu, the Fairview's saloon previously offered a Harding Special cocktail with a near-lethal amount of vodka in it.

Over the years, the Fairview Inn has welcomed a range of famous personalities, including musicians (like John Denver) and adventurers (mountaineers aiming to summit Denali often stay here).

FOUR-LEGGED NATIONAL PARK RANGERS

Why aren't motorized vehicles allowed for wintertime patrols of the third-largest national park?

In the heart of Alaska's vast interior, Denali National Park stretches across 6 million acres of rugged terrain. It's where snow-capped mountains, including the protected land's namesake peak, tower over untouched taiga forests, braided glacial streams, and meadows speckled with fireweed. It's home to grizzly bears, wolves, and caribou, though it's another creature that plays an integral role in preserving this vast wilderness: the sled dog.

For over 100 years, Denali park rangers have used Alaskan huskies to aid in their wintertime patrols. Initially, the pups were needed to help rangers look for poachers, though today their job is more often to do check-ins with people adventuring in the protected land, deliver supplies to remote ranger stations, and assist with scientific projects like measuring snow depth and collecting scat samples to better understand how far the park's animals range.

Not only are the dogs more reliable than snowmobiles (which have a hard time starting in sub-zero temperatures, whereas the pups wake up ready to run), but they're also important for conservation. The 1964 Wilderness Act mandates that no permanent roads may be built in Denali and no motorized vehicles can be used to patrol the vast park, so the sled dogs

---

There are more than 400 national park units across the United States—Denali National Park and Preserve is the only one with dogs on staff.

DENALI NATIONAL PARK SLED DOG KENNELS

Photo courtesy of the National Park Service

WHAT: Where Denali's sled dog teams reside

WHERE: Alaska 3, Denali National Park and Preserve

COST: Fee to enter the park

PRO TIP: Whenever there's a new litter of puppies, they're named around a theme. The Fire Litter, for example, had dogs named Blaze, Char, and Spark.

allow rangers to travel through the protected land without leaving a lasting imprint.

In the summer, the dogs serve as ambassadors to the more than 600,000 people who visit the park between Memorial Day and Labor Day, teaching them about the wild landscapes, the importance of dog sledding in Alaska, and how they're uniquely adapted to do the work. Each dog (with the exception of the puppies, who have their own pen for play and socialization) has its own log cabin–style house with its name on it in the dog yard, where canines wait to participate in dog-sledding demonstrations and receive belly rubs and ear scratches from visitors.

CHERRY, PUMPKIN, OR LEMON MERINGUE

Why is Takotna, a tiny village of 58 people, the favorite stop of mushers on the Iditarod Trail?

Since the inaugural Iditarod Trail Sled Dog Race in 1973, locals in Takotna, a pint-sized checkpoint found 329 miles into the nearly 1,000-mile competition, have dished out made-to-order breakfasts, moose stew, and other free meals to weary mushers. But it's the community's pies that racers remember.

Each year, locals make upwards of 100 pies, a task that starts months before the race, with volunteers flying to Anchorage (no roads lead to Takotna) to buy the necessary crusts and fillings. Then, in the weeks leading up to the race, bakers will make and freeze pies in advance, so they're ready to go when mushers call their teams to a halt.

It was a tradition started by Jan Newton, who held the moniker "The Pie Lady" until her passing in 2012. Her generosity was so appreciated by mushers that she and her husband, Dick, were inducted into the Iditarod Hall of Fame in 2008. The year following her death, she was named the Iditarod's Honorary Musher, an accolade that means the honoree is listed as the first person off the starting line. In a press release that year, the Iditarod staff said of Newton: "Her contributions to the race are remarkable and have elevated her to a position of legendary prominence."

WILLOW LAKE

WHAT: The official start of the Iditarod sled dog race

WHERE: Willow Lake, Willow

COST: Free

PRO TIP: There aren't any hotels in Takotna, so attending the start is usually the easiest way to watch the race.

Jan's friend Nell Huffman has since taken up the Patron Saint of Pies mantle and continues to make sure mushers feel welcome. And they do. During the race, competitors are required to take one 24-hour rest. Because of the outsized generosity of Takotna, roughly half of the mushers declare their break in Takotna to bask in the warmth of the community and its pies.

Each year, the Iditarod opens applications for volunteers to work on the trail, including in Takotna. Veterinarians, aircraft mechanics, and communications personnel are the most sought after.

HELLO, DOLLY

How did a gold rush boomtown bar survive into the 21st century?

During the height of the Klondike Gold Rush, Skagway, a community strategically located at the head of the White Pass and Chilkoot Trails, became a bustling hub for the thousands of hopeful prospectors that streamed into the then territory. Those throngs of men seeking wealth also thirsted for potent potables and entertainment, so the Red Onion, a saloon and bordello, opened to serve the need.

RED ONION SALOON

WHAT: A bar/brothel museum

WHERE: 201 Broadway, Skagway

COST: Varies

PRO TIP: The Red Onion Saloon is only open seasonally, so be sure to check the hours before visiting.

Opened in 1898, the first floor operated as a bar and social gathering space, while the second floor was home to the brothel, with 10 cribs (small rooms) where the madam and her ladies conducted business (each with hidden doors, in case the women needed to make a quick exit). To efficiently manage the women's assignments, dolls representing each lady were placed on the bar. When a woman was engaged with a client, her doll would be laid on its back; once free, the doll would be set upright again.

When the gold rush slowed down, the Red Onion closed its doors. For several decades afterward, the building served various purposes, including a bakery, laundry, military barracks during World War II, and even a television station.

In the 1970s, with growing interest in preserving Alaska's gold rush heritage, the Red Onion Saloon was restored to its former glory. It was reopened as a saloon, complete with a restaurant and a historical museum on the second floor, which pays homage to its colorful past as a brothel. Today, the seasonally open saloon is one of Skagway's most popular

Photo courtesy of the Red Onion Saloon

tourist destinations, known for its lively atmosphere, hearty bar fare, costumed staff, a surprisingly large collection of bedpans used as decor, and exhibits that tell the story of the Red Onion's heyday. Guided tours of the brothel museum offer visitors a glimpse into the lives of the women who worked there, alongside relics and artifacts from the period, ranging from antique hairpins to the actual red lantern that hung outside when Red Onion was part of a larger red-light district.

Red Onion Saloon also offers walking tours of Skagway led by one of their madams. Along the way, the guide shares the history of the infamous characters who spent time in Skagway, from Soapy Smith to Klondike Kate.

DON'T FORGET SOCKS

How did Slate Creek get rechristened as Coldfoot?

A small percentage of those who travel to Alaska make it past the Arctic Circle—doing so garners some serious bragging rights (and, if you're on a tour, usually a certificate). Typically those that do join the rarefied club do so by visiting Coldfoot, the northernmost truck stop in the United States.

THE COLDFOOT CAMP TRUCKER'S CAFE

WHAT: A basic restaurant and gift shop

WHERE: Mile 175, Dalton Hwy., Coldfoot

COST: Free to visit; prices of food and beverages vary

PRO TIP: Coldfoot was made famous by the show *Ice Road Truckers* on the History Channel—you might see some of the characters refueling there.

Situated in the Brooks Mountain Range, Coldfoot (population: 270) serves as a critical pit stop for truckers heading to the remote oil fields of Prudhoe Bay. Like many communities in rural Alaska, Coldfoot has the gold rush to thank for its existence. Prospectors came to the area to pan what was then called Slate Creek. The story goes,

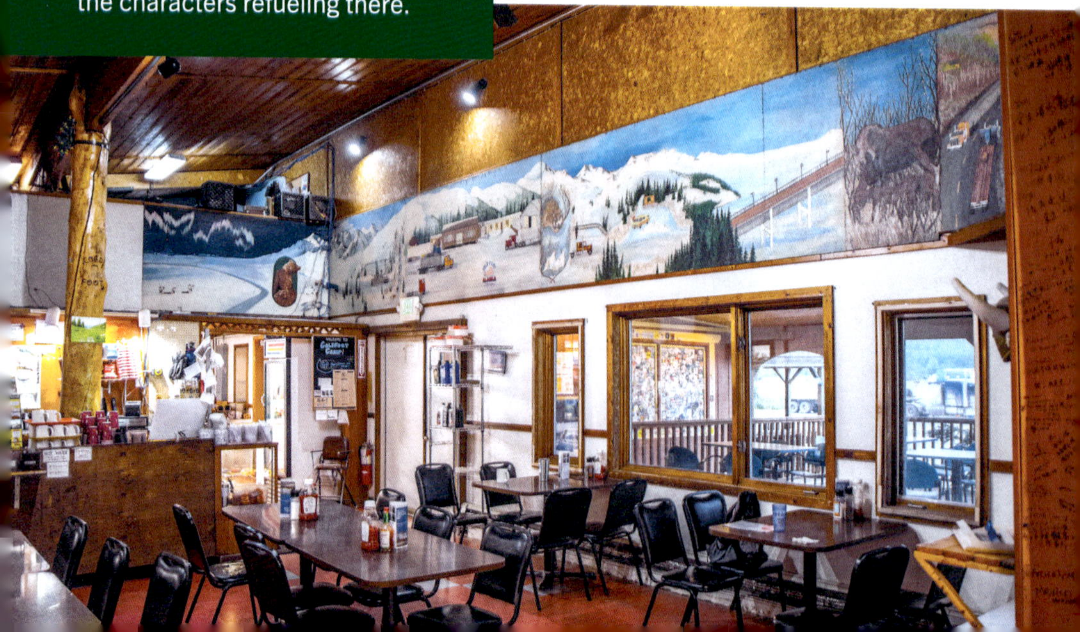

Left: *Coldfoot's one modest cafe and bar.* Above: *The town of Coldfoot.*
Photos courtesy of Coldfoot Camp

the community was renamed after scores of those fortune-seekers got "cold feet" about spending the winter in this frozen expanse and retreated south. By the 1970s, the area was largely abandoned. However, the construction of the Trans-Alaska Pipeline and the opening of the Dalton Highway, also known as the "Haul Road," brought the region back to life. Today the entire town consists of a post office, a troopers' office, a ragtag clutch of old-school gas pumps, a hotel made of trailers that once housed pipeline workers, a barebones restaurant, and a runway for bush planes.

For those not heading to the oil fields, Coldfoot serves as a jumping-off point for visitors to the Gates of the Arctic National Park and the Arctic National Wildlife Refuge, two vast expanses of wilderness devoid of roads or trails, offering a truly unspoiled natural experience for hikers, backpackers, and wildlife enthusiasts. In the winter, aurora chasers come to Coldfoot for a chance to witness the ethereal northern lights dance across the sky.

The Coldfoot Camp also operates one of the most northerly post offices in the United States, reinforcing the community's role as a hub for the sparse population that traverses this northern region.

DOLLAR BILLS AND LIME WEDGES

What's the most expensive way to wallpaper a bar?

The Spit, a 4.5-mile-long finger of land that juts into Kachemak Bay, has long been the focal point for Homer's fishing industry—it's from here that charter boats filled with anglers leave each day in the summer to reel in a trophy salmon or halibut that will inspire "It was THIS BIG" stories for years to come.

And after a day at sea, there's one place on the Spit where guides and rodmen are most likely to gather: the Salty Dawg Saloon.

Originally one of the first cabins in Homer, the Salty Dawg Saloon has had many lives. Over the decades, the structure has been a post office, a coal-mining office, a grocery store, a railroad station, and even a schoolhouse. In 1957, the building was repurposed as a saloon, and a few years later a faux lighthouse was constructed around the building's backup water tower, making it one of the most recognizable buildings in the state.

SALTY DAWG SALOON

WHAT: A historic wood cabin bar with cash from all over the world stapled to the ceiling

WHERE: 4380 Homer Spit Rd., Homer

COST: Prices of drinks vary.

PRO TIP: Ask the bartender for a Sharpie (so you can sign your dollar) and a thumbtack.

The famed watering hole has a distinct character, with low ceilings, wooden beams, a dimly lit interior, and thousands of dollar bills affixed to the walls, ceilings, and any other available surface. It's a tradition that started when local fishermen left money for their buddies still on the water to buy a drink on them later. It evolved into a practice where any visitor can add to the growing tapestry by leaving some currency (often

Photo courtesy of Jorden Perez

inked with their signature or a note). In a 2022 KTUU segment, the saloon manager estimated that there were more than $50,000 worth of bills festooning the bar.

The dollar bills aren't the only relics here—the saloon also proudly displays maritime antiques (many from shipwrecks), historical photographs, and quirky items that reflect Homer's rich fishing culture.

> XTRATUF boots are arguably the most known piece of apparel in Alaska . . . followed by Salty Dawg Saloon sweatshirts, which are sold behind the bar.

BUS 142

Whatever happened to the infamous Magic Bus?

Chances are, if you've heard the story of the "Magic Bus," it's because you've read Jon Krakauer's 1996 book *Into the Wild* or watched the 2007 film adaptation directed by Sean Penn. While the story is long and layered, the gist is that a young adventurer named Chris McCandless (who also went by the pseudonym "Alexander Supertramp") traveled across the country in the early 1990s before heading to Alaska with a goal of living off the land. He hiked down the Stampede Trail near Denali National Park, crossed the frozen Teklanika River, and eventually found a weathered city bus that had been abandoned there. Armed with a .22-caliber rifle, a bag of rice, and limited knowledge of the harsh realities of the Alaskan wilderness, McCandless made the bus his home for 113 days. However, as the spring thaw transformed the landscape, the rivers became impassable, cutting him off from escape, and he tragically died of starvation.

Both the book and the film sparked debate and intrigue about McCandless's motives, his character, and the nature of his death. Some view McCandless as a hero, a modern-day transcendentalist who dared to defy societal norms in search of deeper meaning. For others, his passing represents the dangers of romanticizing the wilderness and underestimating its harshness.

Despite these differing views, the Magic Bus became a pilgrimage site for adventurers, thrill-seekers, and those

---

The bus was once part of the Fairbanks City Transit System and was brought to the wilderness as shelter for workers during a road project in the 1960s and was left there afterward for hunters and travelers.

inspired by McCandless's story. Myriad people trekked into the wild each year to visit the bus, often risking their own safety in the treacherous terrain. In June 2020, due to safety concerns and the growing number of rescue missions, the state decided to airlift Bus 142 from its remote location. The vehicle was taken to a secure facility, with future plans to exhibit it at the Museum of the North in Fairbanks.

49TH STATE BREWING COMPANY, HEALY

WHAT: Where the replica of the "Magic Bus" used in the film *Into the Wild* sits

WHERE: 248 Parks Hwy. 5 Mile, Healy

COST: Free to visit; prices of food and beverages vary

PRO TIP: Check out the photos and literature about McCandless inside the bus

The author and her dog in front of the movie replica of Bus 142. Photo courtesy of Shaun Hanley

A TOWN BUILT ON CHEER

Where do letters to Santa go when sent in Alaska?

It is always the holiday season in North Pole, Alaska. The town's streets bear festive names like Santa Claus Lane and Kris Kringle Drive, the street lights look like candy canes, and a herd of reindeer live outside the Santa Claus House.

SANTA CLAUS HOUSE

WHAT: A Santa-themed gift shop

WHERE: 101 St. Nicholas Dr., North Pole

COST: Free to visit

PRO TIP: Be sure to ask about the Original Letter from Santa while you're there.

Founded in 1952 by Con and Nellie Miller, the Santa Claus House began as a humble trading post. While working one day, a local kid came into the shop and recognized Con, who was known for donning a red suit during the holiday season, and greeted him as Santa. Inspired by the interaction, the Millers renamed the store Santa Claus House. It wasn't until the '70s that the objects within the store started to morph from everyday goods and groceries to the Christmas ornaments, holiday cards, and seasonal decorations that are sold today.

While visiting the store is magical year-round, it's particularly enchanting in the winter. The short days of December mean North Pole is often blanketed in darkness, illuminated by festive lights, and frequently covered in a thick layer of snow. It's also when Santa holds court, allowing local and visiting kids to sit on his lap and share their Christmas wishes with him.

Photo courtesy of Santa Claus House

Many of the letters written to Santa in Alaska end up here, too—there's a wall of some of the many missives to Old Saint Nick in the store. And year-round, guests can send letters from Father Christmas to loved ones anywhere in the world, complete with the North Pole postmark.

The giant Santa outside the store had to be driven from Anchorage in four pieces so it could fit under overpasses on the Parks Highway.

SO CLOSE, YET SO FAR

How many miles actually separate Alaska and Russia?

Contrary to what many people believe, former Alaska Governor Sarah Palin never said the famous line, "I can see Russia from my house." This phrase was actually spoken by actress and comedian Tina Fey during a skit on *Saturday Night Live* in 2008. However, it's indeed possible to see Russia from one small island in Alaska.

Found in the icy waters of the Bering Strait, 16 miles west of mainland Alaska's Seward Peninsula, is Little Diomede. And just 2.4 miles further west, across the International Date Line, is Big Diomede, an island held by Russia.

The border between the two islands was first drawn in 1867, when the United States purchased Alaska from a cash-strapped Russia. Then the Treaty of Cession placed the easternmost island, Little Diomede, under American control, while Big Diomede remained part of Russia. Still, for the Iñupiat families who had been moving between the two islands for centuries, the border was largely ignored.

That is until 1948, when the Cold War prompted Russia to turn Big Diomede into a military base and all Indigenous inhabitants were relocated to Siberia. Many of the families never saw their relatives again.

Though the two Diomede Islands are just 2.4 miles apart, there is a 21-hour time difference between them.

Little Diomede in the foreground. Photo courtesy of Casey Anderson

Today, Big Diomede remains uninhabited, while Little Diomede is home to roughly 100 people. Though the two Diomede Islands are just 2.4 miles apart, there is a 21-hour time difference between them, which is why Big Diomede is sometimes called Tomorrow Island, while Little Diomede is Yesterday Island.

LITTLE DIOMEDE NATIVE STORE

WHAT: A grocery store and one of the only businesses on Little Diomede

WHERE: Walrus Dr., Little Diomede

COST: Free to visit; prices of goods vary

PRO TIP: While you can buy food and goods here, it's better to come to Little Diomede with your own supplies—prices tend to be significantly higher in rural Alaska.

A LUNAR LANDSCAPE ON EARTH

What happens when a volcano erupts for 60 straight hours?

Hidden in the remote wilderness of Katmai National Park lies one of the most otherworldly landscapes on Earth: the Valley of Ten Thousand Smokes.

It's an area born from one of the largest volcanic eruptions in recorded history. In 1912, the Novarupta Volcano exploded with such incredible force that it completely changed the landscape. Nearby rivers were choked with ash, altering water courses, and vast forests were destroyed, leaving barren expanses. The ashfall from the eruption, which was hundreds of feet deep in some areas, blanketed wilderness as far away as Kodiak Island, affecting wildlife habitats and ecosystems for years.

When the eruption stopped, heat was still trapped within that thick layer of volcanic ash. As groundwater and surface water seeped through the cinders and came into contact with

the hot ground below, the water vaporized and rose through the debris in plumes of steam. From a distance, it looked like there were thousands of smoke columns coming through the charred land—hence the name "Valley of Ten Thousand Smokes."

Over time, the fumaroles disappeared as the area cooled, but the name remains to describe this extraordinary volcanic landscape. The altered topography makes the area look so much like a lunar landscape that NASA astronauts have used it for training missions. Even today, scientists routinely use the area as a natural laboratory for studying volcanic processes and ecological recovery.

ROBERT F. GRIGGS VISITOR CENTER

WHAT: The visitor center closest to the Valley of Ten Thousand Smokes at Katmai National Park

WHERE: 23 miles from Brooks Camp on the only road within the national park

COST: Free to visit

PRO TIP: It's possible to join a ranger-led tour of the area from this visitor center.

Photos courtesy of the National Park Service

In 1916, a scientist named Robert F. Griggs led an expedition supported by the National Geographic Society. His findings helped get Katmai recognized as a national park.

ALASKA'S FAVORITE CRACKER

How did a military ration become part of Alaska's food culture?

Whether topped with smoked salmon, smeared with fireweed jelly, heaped with herring eggs, or crumbled into moose stew, many meals in rural Alaska aren't complete without a slab of Sailor Boy Pilot Bread. In fact, of all the Sailor Boy Pilot Bread eaten worldwide, 98 percent is consumed in Alaska.

Made of flour, salt, and water, these dense saucer-sized crackers are derived from hardtack, a long-lasting type of survival bread. Hardtack has origins in the seafaring world—sailors on years-long expeditions needed food that could withstand the test of time and harsh conditions, and the dense biscuits were a reliable source of sustenance on round-the-world journeys, thanks to their long shelf life, low moisture content, and simplicity. For those same reasons, these later became a staple in military rations.

COSTCO

WHAT: One of the places you'll always find Sailor Boy Pilot Bread for sale

WHERE: 330 W Dimond Blvd., Anchorage

COST: Varies

PRO TIP: Look for the blue-and-white boxes on a pallet near the front of the store.

As more people began venturing north in the late 1800s, they found themselves needing similar solutions to sustain them in the rugged and remote landscape of Alaska. For more than a century, Sailor Boy Pilot Bread has been a vital food for people living in more rural communities, where grocery stores can be few and far between—and where supplies come in by bush plane or boat. Sailor Boy Pilot Bread can last for years, making it a pantry staple that families rely on in lean times,

Photo courtesy of Sailor Boy Pilot Bread

during harsh winters, or when supply routes are cut off by bad weather.

But Sailor Boy Pilot Bread is not just about practicality; it has also become a cherished part of Alaskan culture. Many Alaskans have fond memories of childhood meals made with pilot bread, and it often shows up at community potlucks, Native gatherings, and on camping excursions. For some, it is associated with long hunting and fishing trips, where the simplicity of a pilot bread meal provided comfort in the wilderness.

The shelf life of Sailor Boy Pilot Bread is 10 years, though if kept dry, it can last far longer than that.

AN ARCHITECTURAL ODDITY

What would make you pull over the car 20 miles from Denali National Park?

Alaska isn't one for quirky roadside attractions—you won't find massive fiberglass animals or head-scratching art pieces here. However, there is one bizarre exception.

Situated along the Parks Highway, just outside of Cantwell and surrounded by towering spruce trees, rolling hills, and snow-capped peaks, is Igloo City. Though its name might conjure images of a thriving Arctic community, this "city" is actually a single, weather-worn, four-story igloo.

IGLOO CITY

WHAT: A ginormous concrete igloo

WHERE: Mile 188.5, Parks Hwy., near Cantwell

COST: Free to visit

PRO TIP: While the igloo itself is boarded up, you can still stop and take pictures of it.

The white, dome-shaped building with dormer windows was the brainchild of local developer Leon Smith, who had grand plans in the 1970s to build what he believed would be an iconic hotel catering to tourists heading to nearby Denali National Park and Preserve. He planned to have 58 guest rooms, a restaurant, bar, liquor store, and gift shop on the property, as well as a penthouse suite for himself.

However, the hotel never officially opened. Due to structural and code violations, construction ceased on the 80-foot-tall, 105-foot-wide building well before it could be completed. In the mid-'90s, the building was sold to a man named Brad Fisher, who ran a gas station adjacent to the property for roughly a decade.

Photos courtesy of Dawson Little

Today, this massive concrete igloo, with its deteriorating and graffiti-covered facade, remains uninhabited. Still, the building's eerie presence has a certain charm, and despite its unfinished state, Igloo City has indeed become a tourist attraction—just not the one its founder envisioned.

Igloo City was sold in 2023 to a family who plan to turn it into a distillery, if they can get it up to code.

THERE'S GOLD IN THOSE HILLS

What would cause a prolific gold mine to close?

With its rolling meadows dappled with wildflowers, alpine lakes, peaks that seem to poke the sky, and opportunities for viewing wildlife ranging from moose to marmots, Hatcher Pass is an incredible destination for nature lovers. It's also exceptional for history buffs, thanks to the Independence Mine.

Once one of the largest gold-mining operations in Alaska, the Independence Mine was established in the early 1900s, and at its height, more than 200 workers lived on-site.

Independence Mine closed during World War II, as the focus on national resources shifted away from gold production. After a brief resurgence post-war, the mine finally ceased operations in 1951, leaving behind the ghostly ruins of the mess halls, bunkhouses, and processing mills we see today.

Visitors to Independence Mine today can explore several well-preserved buildings, many of which have been restored as part of the state historical park. The interpretive displays and guided tours bring the past to life, explaining not only the history of the mine but also the challenges faced by the miners and their families in such a remote and unforgiving location.

INDEPENDENCE MINE STATE HISTORICAL PARK VISITOR CENTER

WHAT: The Mine Manager's House, which now serves as the visitor center for the abandoned gold mine

WHERE: 23264 Gold Cord Rd., Palmer

COST: Fees for parking and guided tours (though self-led tours are free)

PRO TIP: Check out the simulated mining tunnel and displays on gold-mining methods.

Photos courtesy of Tom Bol Photography/Mat-Su CBV

The mine is typically open to visitors from June to September when the snow has melted and the site is most accessible. However, winter visitors can still explore the site on foot or skis, though access to buildings may be limited due to snow.

Since Independence Mine was made a historical park in 1980, the state has been working to restore the buildings and tunnels for tourism, making it one of the better places to get an understanding of Alaska's mining past.

SHAKE, RATTLE, AND ROLL

EARTHQUAKE PARK

WHAT: A greenspace popular for walking, biking, and cross-country skiing

WHERE: 5101 Point Woronzof Rd., Anchorage

COST: Free to visit

PRO TIP: Earthquake Park terminates at Point Woronzof, near Ted Stevens Anchorage International Airport, making it an excellent spot for plane watching.

When and where was the largest-ever earthquake in North America?

At first glance, Earthquake Park may seem like just another peaceful green space—it's part of the larger Coastal Trail system, making it a popular destination for walkers, cyclists, and cross-country skiers. However, if you look closely, you can still see signs of a 1964 earthquake that changed the landscape of Anchorage forever.

On March 27, 1964, at 5:36 p.m., Alaska was rocked by the most powerful earthquake ever recorded in North American

Earthquake Park, blanketed in snow

A sidewalk in Earthquake Park depicting the damage done. Photo courtesy of Brittney Patton

history—a magnitude 9.2 quake that shook the state for nearly five minutes. Known as the Good Friday Earthquake, it caused widespread destruction across southern Alaska. Some areas near Kodiak were permanently raised by 30 feet, and Valdez became so unsteady the entire town had to be moved.

Anchorage was the city closest to the epicenter and where Earthquake Park now stands. A coastal neighborhood known as Turnagain Heights was particularly affected due to its clay soil composition. As the earthquake struck, the unstable ground gave way in a massive landslide, pulling entire streets and more than 75 houses into the inlet, permanently scarring the land with massive fissures.

Today, Earthquake Park stands as a memorial to the lives lost and the homes destroyed. The interpretive signs and markers along the trails detail the science behind the earthquake, explaining how the shifting tectonic plates below Alaska created such a powerful force.

Alaska is one of the most seismically active regions in the world. Of the 10 strongest earthquakes ever recorded, three have occurred in Alaska, and each year approximately 5,000 earthquakes happen, including 1,000 that measure above 3.5 on the Richter scale.

BURNING MAN, ALASKA STYLE

What happens when thousands of Alaskans gather in the mountains for a winter festival?

Every April, Alaska's remote Hoodoo Mountains come alive with Arctic Man, one of the most extreme winter sports events in the world. The main event, the Arctic Man Ski & Sno-Go Classic, is a unique blend of skiing (or snowboarding) and snowmachining (snowmobiling to Lower 48ers) that tests the limits of both man and machine. Competitors work in teams: a skier or snowboarder starts at the top of a 5,800-foot peak and descends at breakneck speeds. At the halfway point, the racer grabs onto a towrope connected to their snowmachining teammate, who then rockets them up the next hill, reaching speeds of over 90 mph before releasing them for a final descent to the finish line. It's the thrilling combination of speed and precision that makes Arctic Man a jaw-dropping spectacle. And because the entry fee pays the winning team, often tens of thousands of dollars, the contest even attracts professional athletes and Olympians.

But it's not just about the competition. The weeklong event draws a massive crowd, with thousands of RVs, snowmachines, and trailers turning the otherwise desolate tundra into a buzzing, temporary village. Revelers set up impromptu races, mini-events, and tailgating parties on the snow by day, and arrange for live music, bonfires, and fireworks that keep the party going well into the long northern nights, giving Arctic Man the atmosphere of an extreme sports event, a music festival, and a winter camping adventure all rolled into one.

The fastest time for completing the 5.5-mile course was just under four minutes.

ARCTIC MAN

WHAT: A springtime snowmachining extravaganza

WHERE: Mile 198.5, Richardson Hwy.

COST: Fee for competing; free to watch

PRO TIP: Bring everything you need—it's a jaunt to the closest town.

Photo courtesy of Tom Bol Photography/Mat-Su CBV

CULTURAL PRESERVATION IN A MODERN CONTEXT

Where can you learn about all of Alaska's Indigenous populations at once?

Alaska is home to 229 federally recognized tribes (almost half of the total number of tribal groups in the country) and dozens of distinct Native languages, reflecting an extraordinary diversity of traditions, stories, and ways of life.

And though Anchorage sits on the traditional homelands of the Dena'ina Athabascan people, you can learn about all major Indigenous groups in the 49th state at the Alaska Native Heritage Center.

The Heritage Center explores more than 10,000 years of Indigenous history, culture, dance, and art through interactive exhibits and live demonstrations. Inside you'll find the Hall of Cultures, where visitors can explore exhibits on the clothing and tools Indigenous people traditionally used, as well as contemporary art and design.

Outside are a half dozen Village Sites, where guests can peek into historical dwellings from various Native groups. Each site is a full-scale reconstruction, allowing visitors to step into an Iñupiat qargi (community house), a Yup'ik sod house, or a Tlingit clan house, among others. Knowledgeable Alaska Native guides provide interpretations and demonstrations,

---

Be sure to check out the ANHC's Ch'k'iqadi Gallery, the only Alaska Native–owned and –operated gift shop in Anchorage. There, artists are working to redefine and invent new art with traditional practices.

ALASKA NATIVE HERITAGE CENTER

WHAT: A cultural center that offers an in-depth look at Indigenous life in Alaska

WHERE: 8800 Heritage Center Dr., Anchorage

COST: Prices vary for children, adults, seniors, and Alaska residents.

PRO TIP: Check the schedule for cultural performances—the demonstrations of sports played at the World Indigenous Games is particularly interesting.

bringing the history and daily rituals of these communities to life.

The Alaska Native Heritage Center is not just a tourist destination; it is a vital resource for education and community engagement. The center partners with schools across the state, providing educational materials, curriculum guides, and field trip opportunities that integrate Alaska Native perspectives into learning. Special events like Native Youth Olympics, artist residencies, hands-on workshops that invite visitors to learn traditional skills (such as beading, weaving, carving, or Native cooking), and summer camps for children immerse participants in Indigenous traditions, fostering cultural pride and connection among Native youth.

UP, UP, AND AWAY

Why are bush planes so important to rural Alaska?

Alaska has 16 times more aircraft and six times as many pilots per capita than anywhere else in the country. A big part of the reason behind that is how challenging it is to reach rural areas. More than 200 communities in Alaska (82 percent of the state) don't have roads that connect them. Unless you want to hike, go by dog sled, or travel there by boat, chances are you'll need to take a bush plane to get to these off-the-road system villages.

And to Alaskans, these planes are not just a mode of transportation. They are a lifeline. They connect people, deliver supplies, and open

ALASKA AVIATION MUSEUM

WHAT: A museum with multiple hangars of exhibits on Alaska aviation history, as well as vintage aircraft

WHERE: 4721 Aircraft Dr., Anchorage

COST: Prices vary for children, adults, and seniors

PRO TIP: Don't miss the flight simulator exhibit.

A Grumman G-21 Goose landing on Lake Hood. Photos courtesy of the Alaska Air Museum

up access to some of the most hard-to-reach and breathtaking landscapes on earth. Simply put, they knit Alaska together.

One of the best places to learn about Alaska's aviation history is the Alaska Aviation Museum. The museum boasts an impressive collection of over 30 historic aircraft, many of which were instrumental in Alaska's development. One of the star attractions is the Grumman G-21 Goose, an amphibious aircraft that allows travel across both land and water. Visitors will also find the Curtiss P-40 Warhawk, a symbol of Alaska's involvement in World War II when Anchorage and other parts of the state became critical defense points against potential invasion. The museum brings the stories of Alaska's legendary bush pilots to life, with artifacts and personal accounts that highlight their daring exploits, often flying solo into the wilderness to deliver crucial supplies to isolated villages.

The Alaska Aviation Museum is located on Lake Hood, home of the largest and busiest seaplane base in the world.

AN EXTRA SERVING OF VEGETABLES

Why do plants grow so big in Alaska?

The average size of an adult black rhinoceros is roughly 2,147 pounds. It's also the weight of the heaviest pumpkin ever entered into the Alaska State Fair. Among its portly record-holding peers are a 42.75-pound beet, a 63.3-pound stalk of celery, a 138.25-pound cabbage, and a 168.6-pound watermelon, just to name a few.

The fair itself, founded in 1936, was initially a small local celebration in the town of Palmer, in the fertile Matanuska-Susitna Valley. The US government had encouraged settlers, particularly from the Midwest, to move to this area during the Great Depression, and these early farmers discovered that even though Alaska has a relatively short growing season, the long days (nearly 24 hours in some regions) in the summer supercharge the growth of produce. The pumpkins, for instance, can pack on up to 25 pounds a day, if the conditions are right. Over time, the state fair became a platform for showcasing these natural wonders.

Of the vegetables, pumpkins and cabbages tend to garner the most excitement—they often need teams of people to lift them onto the scale on the weigh-in day. But each time a vegetable surpasses the weight of another, the crowd cheers.

ALASKA STATE FAIR

WHAT: An annual two-week festival featuring record-setting vegetables, concerts, games, and food

WHERE: 2075 Glenn Hwy., Palmer

COST: Varies

PRO TIP: The fair can get crowded, especially on weekends. Arriving early will give you the best parking options and shorter lines for rides, food, and events.

Photos courtesy of Tom Bol Photography/ Mat-Su CBV

The corpulent veggies are kept on display throughout the rest of the fair for fans to admire, and afterward they're donated to local farmers to help feed livestock.

A 96.95-pound kohlrabi that was entered in the competition in 2006 still holds the world record.

FISH ON!

Where can you fish for king salmon in the middle of downtown?

If you're standing near Ship Creek in downtown Anchorage and you hear someone call "Fish on!" it is a good idea to get out of the way. While most of the king salmon that come out of this riverway are between 20 to 25 pounds on average, some top out at more than 50 pounds—and they're not going to give up the fight to get to their spawning grounds easily.

Ship Creek is the only urban king salmon fishery in the world. It's also incredibly prolific, and anyone, locals and visitors alike, can try to land one of the massive fish that swim up the waterway each season. It is estimated that around 3,800 kings (also known as Chinook salmon) are pulled from these chilly waters each June. Then, later in the summer, it's also possible to catch coho (otherwise known as silver salmon). And while filling the freezer for winter is enough for some, others are in it for a possible payday. Each June, The Bait Shack hosts the Slam'n Salm'n Derby, where prize money (and an authentic Alaskan gold nugget) is awarded to the anglers who reel in the largest king (there are separate categories for men, women, military, and children), and a Coho Rodeo Derby in July, where rodmen try to land the heftiest silver. Some of the proceeds from the events go toward supporting various Alaska nonprofit organizations.

THE BAIT SHACK

WHAT: A stand selling most the necessary gear for angling

WHERE: 212 W Whitney Rd., Anchorage

COST: Varies depending on what supplies are needed

PRO TIP: Don't forget to get your sport fishing license ahead of time.

You don't have to fish to enjoy the action, though. Both the banks and the bridges spanning the river are good spots to

Photo courtesy of Brittney Patton

watch the anglers work. And because the water is so clear, you'll often be able to see just how close the fishermen were to landing a trophy fish.

The popularity of Ship Creek means anglers are often standing shoulder to shoulder in the waterway. Locals call it "combat fishing."

NATURE'S LIGHT SHOW

Why is Alaska the best place to see the northern lights in the United States?

The shimmering curtains of light that pirouette across the night sky in waves of chartreuse, violet, crimson, and magenta are known as the *aurora borealis*, or more simply, the northern lights.

Today we know that they're caused when electrically charged particles from the sun collide with the Earth's atmosphere. Before, however, Alaska's Indigenous people created stories to try to demystify the solar show. In the northern parts of the state, the Iñupiat people believed the undulating ribbons to be a bad omen and carried weapons to protect themselves when the lights were out. In interior Alaska, the Athabascan people considered the luminescence to be more positive—they thought the spectacle was the spirits of animals they'd harvested, like moose and salmon.

Fairbanks is one of the best places to see the northern lights in Alaska—the city is known for having more than 200 auroral appearances each year.

Northern lights most often appear in shades of green. Photos courtesy of the National Park Service

CHENA HOT SPRINGS RESORTS

WHAT: A resort with hot springs that's renowned for being a good place to see the northern lights

WHERE: 17600 Chena Hot Springs Rd., Fairbanks

COST: Prices vary for overnight stays and hot spring access.

PRO TIP: The lights typically come out after midnight in Alaska, so plan to stay up late.

Either way, Alaska is one of the best places in the world to see the celestial streamers of light, thanks to its position under the auroral oval. This band encircles the earth's magnetic poles, where the chances of seeing the northern lights are highest. This oval is not stationary; it shifts and expands based on solar activity, but it consistently covers the latitudes where Alaska lies, meaning aurora activity is frequent and intense.

While the lights are technically happening all year, it's only dark enough to witness them from August to April (and that's only if the sky is clear of clouds and there's no competing light pollution). And though scientists can estimate how likely a performance will be on a given night (on a scale of 0 to 9 called the Kp-index), there's no guarantee. It's all a matter of luck.

IN CELEBRATION OF SLUSH

Why does the most popular spring event in Alaska involve icy water?

How do you ring in spring in a ski town? At Alyeska Resort in Girdwood, it involves donning an outrageous costume, ranging from hot dogs to Chewbacca, strapping into skis or onto a snowboard, bombing downhill, and attempting to skim across a pond filled with barely above-freezing water.

It's part of the Spring Carnival, the closing weekend of Alyeska's winter season, and an annual celebration of transitioning into the warmer months. While the festival sees food trucks, beer gardens, downhill mountain bike races, tugs of war, and live bands, the marquee event is Slush Cup, the audacious pond-skimming competition.

The event starts the day before with a costume contest, with the best outfits earning one of the 50 entry slots. On the day of, competitors point and send down the mountain, hoping to build enough speed to glide across a 90-foot watery obstacle. Oh, and there's a smaller pool and a snowy jump ahead of the main slushy basin, as if getting across it wasn't challenging enough.

Most of the competitors wipe out or sink before reaching the far side of the water obstacle, but each year a few make it all the way across. Contestants are judged on a variety of

---

Despite the slush, Alyeska's ski slopes remain open during the Spring Carnival, allowing skiers and snowboarders to enjoy some of the last runs of the season while also partaking in the festivities.

ALYESKA RESORT

WHAT: The only resort attached to the skiing mountain

WHERE: 1000 Arlberg Ave., Girdwood

COST: Slush Cup is free to attend; other activities have fees.

PRO TIP: If you get chilly, visit the Nordic Spa—it is open to nonguests of the hotel.

factors, including costume, best trick, biggest air, and gnarliest wipeout. Traditionally, the winner received a free lift pass to Alyeska Resort for the entire next season (though in some years they have also been able to choose airline vouchers anywhere Alaska Airlines flies).

RUDOLPH AND ALL HIS FRIENDS

Why does sunscreen make you invisible to reindeer?

If you ask Jane Atkinson, the owner of Running Reindeer Ranch in Fairbanks, how she ended up with a herd of reindeer, she'll tell you it's what happens when you live in Alaska and won't let your daughter get a pony.

She'll also explain that the animal's hair is hollow; they don't bite or kick; the clicking noise we hear isn't their hoofs, rather the tendons in their legs; and the same ultraviolet vision that allows them to see through the snow to find lichen, their preferred treat, makes it hard for them to see through sunscreen.

> **RUNNING REINDEER RANCH**
>
> **WHAT:** A unique chance to walk with reindeer
>
> **WHERE:** 1470 Ivans Alley, Fairbanks
>
> **COST:** Varies
>
> **PRO TIP:** Check their website, runningreindeer.com, for their occasional yoga with reindeer classes.

The facts do little to dispel the mystique of the domesticated caribou. If anything, they make the animals seem more fanciful. The family got their first pair of reindeer, Ruby and Moon, in 2007 and more recently have been leading guided two-and-a-half-hour-long walks through the boreal forest on their property, with a goal of teaching travelers about the real-life animals that they might otherwise only associate with fictional holiday stories. The walks are available all summer long and select days in the winter.

All outings start with a safety talk. The biggest takeaways: don't touch their antlers, and if they run toward you, "be a tree" and don't move. The latter is an important note because soon after the reindeer are released from their pen, they eagerly

A reindeer eating lichen

bound down the path to come mingle with the group. If it's spring, some of the females might have calves in tow. After a little meet and greet, wherein guests learn the names and personalities of the current herd members, like Bramble, Forest, and Heather, guests head out for a walk with the reindeer.

Another option for reindeer viewing is the Running Farm in Palmer. There, guests can feed the reindeer pellets and meet other animals, such as moose and musk oxen.

ICY WHAT YOU DID THERE

How do you turn a block of ice into art?

The ice harvested from lakes and ponds around Fairbanks is so clear and bright that it has been exported as far as the Bahamas and Israel. However, its gemlike qualities are also appreciated at home.

Each February, Fairbanks hosts the World Ice Art Championships, also known as Ice Alaska. The event started in 1990 as a one-week, eight-team competition and has evolved into what is considered to be the most prestigious ice-sculpting competition in the world. It's not just about creating sculptures—it's about pushing the boundaries of what's possible with ice.

Artists are given ice blocks, which can weigh as much as 2,000 pounds, and with tools ranging from chisels and saws to blow torches and fine picks, they bring their creations to life.

The sculptures are often delicate, featuring themes ranging from mythology and fantasy to wildlife and more abstract

FAIRBANKS ICE MUSEUM

WHAT: A museum housing massive ice sculptures that operates the rest of the year.

WHERE: 500 2nd Ave., Fairbanks

COST: Fees apply

PRO TIP: During the summer, resident ice artists teach visitors how to sculpt ice themselves.

The competition is the largest of its kind and attracts sculptors from around the world. On average, more than 100 carvers who have built their careers on ice art, from roughly 30 countries, attend.

forms. Some of the previous gallery-worthy pieces have included a spindly armed octopus, a knight fighting a dragon, and the Mad Hatter's tea party, just to name a few.

Artists work around the clock, battling freezing temperatures, sometimes as low as minus 40 degrees Fahrenheit, and the ever-present risk of their creations cracking or collapsing. There are two primary competition categories: Single Block and Multi-Block. The Single Block category gives each artist a limited amount of ice to work with, often leading to intensely detailed and creative designs. The Multi-Block category allows teams to use multiple blocks of ice, resulting in colossal sculptures that can soar over 20 feet tall.

Throughout the competition and for weeks afterward, this frozen wonderland is open to the public and features not only the sculptures but also ice slides, ice mazes, and interactive ice art for visitors to enjoy.

ALONE IN THE WILDERNESS

Why is Gates of the Arctic the least visited national park?

Stretching 13,238 square miles across most of Alaska's Arctic Circle is Gates of the Arctic National Park. It got its name from wilderness advocate Robert Marshall, who traveled in this region in the 1930s and who described two striking peaks, Frigid Crags and Boreal Mountain, as the gates from the Brooks Range into the far north Arctic. And it's true; the duo create a dramatic entrance into a wilderness home to wild rivers, ribbons of unnamed granite peaks more than 7,000 feet tall, valleys chiseled into existence by glaciers, a herd of more than 200,000 caribou, as well as substantial musk ox and bird populations. Combined with the adjacent Kobuk Valley National Park and Noatak National Preserve, these lands are one of the largest protected areas in the world.

And though it's a spectacular landscape and the second-largest national park in the country, Gates of the Arctic holds the title of the least-visited national park in the United States—in a typical year, only about 10,000 people visit this remote parkland. By contrast, more than 4.5 million people visit Grand Canyon National Park each year.

The challenge of getting there is what contributes to low visitation numbers. No roads go to the parkland, so flying in is

ANAKTUVUK PASS RANGER STATION

WHAT: A seasonal visitor center outside Gates of the Arctic park that is staffed by national park rangers

WHERE: 3030 Main St., Anaktuvuk Pass

COST: Free to visit

PRO TIP: This station can provide information on terrain and backcountry camping requirements—but you'd better come prepared, as there is no infrastructure in the protected land.

Photos courtesy of the National Park Service

necessary to visit. There are also no paved roads, trails, visitor centers, or campsites in the park, so wilderness know-how is essential. But those who make the trek are rewarded by being surrounded by truly untouched nature, where the silence is broken only by the sounds of flowing rivers and the occasional call of wildlife.

Snow falls between eight and nine months of the year on average in Gates of the Arctic National Park (though it has been recorded in every month of the year).

THREE BEARS

Where can you see polar bears in Alaska?

Alaska is one of the only places in the world where it is possible to see black bears, brown bears, and polar bears. It's even possible to see all of them in Anchorage—though the only two polar bears live at the Alaska Zoo and are named Cranberry and Kova.

In the wild, humans are most likely to come into contact with black and brown bears—they can be found throughout the state, with few exceptions.

Polar bears, however, are limited to coastal areas above the Arctic Circle and on the North Slope tundra area at the foothills of the Brooks Range. It is estimated that there are between 4,000 and 7,000 polar bears in Alaska. Seeing one of these powerful predators is impressive—adult males average between 600 and 1,200 pounds (though the largest can exceed 1,700 pounds), while adult females weigh between 400 and 700 pounds.

UTQIAGVIK

WHAT: The northernmost city in Alaska, where polar bears are frequently seen

WHERE: Utqiagvik

COST: Free to explore

PRO TIP: It's a good idea to hire an experienced guide for safety reasons if you're keen on seeing polar bears.

Photo courtesy of the National Park Service

Spotting one in nature can be a challenge—and not just because they blend in so well with their surroundings. They spend most of their lives on sea ice, and in winter months, their range is wide—they can be found as far south as St. Lawrence Island and occasionally the Yukon–Kuskokwim Delta. Those keen on spotting one have a better chance during the ice-free period between August and October. Two communities, Kaktovik and Utqiagvik (formerly called Barrow), offer the best, albeit limited, opportunities for observing the ursids. There are also two national park units, Bering Land Bridge National Preserve and Cape Krusenstern National Monument, where sightings have been reported of these icons of the Arctic.

Polar bears are listed as threatened under the Endangered Species Act because the sea ice they depend on for hunting, feeding, and moving around is increasingly diminishing.

BIRDS OF A FEATHER

How many bald eagles can you see at one time?

Each fall, thousands of bald eagles descend on Haines, Alaska, for one reason: to feast.

In October and November, the waterways in the nearby 48,000-acre Alaska Chilkat Bald Eagle Preserve become choked with late-season chum and coho salmon, a critical food source for birds of prey throughout the region. At any given time, up to 3,000 raptors can be roosting in bare treetops, standing on boulders along the shore, or circling high above, waiting for or devouring their meals. Together they make up the largest congregation of bald eagles in the United States.

During the peak salmon run, Haines and the American Bald Eagle Foundation host the annual Alaska Bald Eagle Festival. The weeklong event attracts photographers and bird-watchers from all over the world and gives them a front-row seat to one of nature's most spectacular birding events. The fête features transportation from the city center to prime eagle-viewing spots, educational programming, guided hikes, live music, games, and more.

Throughout the rest of the year, roughly 400 bald eagles call the Alaska Chilkat Bald Eagle Preserve home, and many stick around through February to nosh on the carcasses that pile up along the shore, so chances are good visitors will see America's national bird while visiting at any point of the year. You might also see Alaska's state bird, the willow ptarmigan, though they are not as commonly observed as the bald eagles.

Tens of thousands of eagles live in Alaska, particularly in marine zones and river valleys.

AMERICAN BALD EAGLE FOUNDATION

WHAT: A museum and raptor center

WHERE: 113 Haines Hwy., Haines

COST: Prices vary for children, adults, and active military members.

PRO TIP: Check the schedule for raptor demonstrations.

Photo courtesy of Tom Ganner/Visit Haines

FLIPPERS AND FINS

What goes into saving Alaska's orphaned sea creatures?

Whenever a sea otter, seal, walrus, or other marine animal is found injured, stranded, or orphaned in the 49th state, the Alaska SeaLife Center gets a call. Nestled along the picturesque shores of Resurrection Bay in Seward, the center has more than 4,000 aquatic creatures, including several species of seals, some sea lions, myriad fish, and a flock of marine birds from puffins to guillemots. But it's more than just an aquarium. It's a center for education, research, and rehabilitation.

As the only facility in the state that can provide medical care for aquatic animals, the SeaLife Center brings needy marine life into its care with the goal of eventually releasing them back into the wild. Whenever the animal can't be released, either because of regulations or because they missed out on

---

The Alaska SeaLife Center was built in 1998 using funds from the tragic *Exxon Valdez* oil spill.

Pushki, a baby sea otter who was rehabilitated at the SeaLife Center

learning critical survival skills from Mom, they become permanent residents of the center or, more frequently, another aquarium or zoo with the hope that they'll act as an ambassador for conservation.

The SeaLife Center is also a leading research institution. Its scientists study marine ecosystems to understand the effects of climate change, pollution, and human activity on wildlife. The center's research helps inform conservation strategies aimed at preserving Alaska's vulnerable species.

The center is open throughout the year for visitors, who can engage in hands-on exhibits and presentations that highlight the importance of marine life and what can be done to protect it.

ALASKA SEALIFE CENTER

WHAT: Alaska's only permanent marine mammal rehabilitation facility.

WHERE: 301 Railway Ave., Seward

COST: Varies for children and adults

PRO TIP: Be sure to visit the touch tank.

CARIBOU AND SAND DUNES

What makes Kobuk Valley one of the most fascinating national parks?

Twice a year, one of the last great large mammal migrations on Earth happens in Alaska. More than half a million caribou make the roughly 800-mile trek following the ancient route from their wintering grounds to their breeding grounds and back again. No other land animal travels that distance.

It happens in the remote wilderness of northwestern Alaska's Kobuk Valley National Park. Spanning over 1.7 million acres, the protected land is filled with rugged mountains, sprawling river valleys, dense boreal forests, and one of the most unexpected sights in the Arctic: towering sand dunes.

Covering 25 square miles, these golden waves rise dramatically from the surrounding tundra, creating a surreal, desert-like landscape that feels as if it belongs in an entirely different world.

The sand, created by the grinding of ancient glaciers, was carried to the Kobuk Valley by winds and water. Visiting offers travelers the unique experience of walking barefoot on the sand while being surrounded by snowy peaks and Arctic wilderness. And just like Katmai National Park's Valley of Ten Thousand Smokes, Kobuk

NORTHWEST ARCTIC HERITAGE CENTER

WHAT: The main visitor center for the Western Arctic National Parklands (Kobuk Valley National Park, Cape Krusenstern National Monument, and Noatak National Preserve)

WHERE: 171 Third Ave., Kotzebue

COST: Free to visit

PRO TIP: If needed, the visitor center can help with trip planning and has bear-resistant food containers for loan.

Valley was used by NASA for training programs (in this case, to better understand the environment of Mars).

The park is inaccessible by road and can be reached only by plane or boat, making it a pristine destination for adventurers seeking solitude and untouched beauty. Visitors to Kobuk Valley can explore the park's rugged terrain by hiking, backpacking, or paddling the meandering Kobuk River.

Archaeological evidence shows that humans have been living in the Kobuk Valley for at least 12,000 years. Many of these early peoples followed the caribou herds, just like the modern Iñupiat people do today.

Photo courtesy of the National Park Service

ALL CAUGHT UP

What is the most egalitarian way to get a freezer full of salmon in Alaska?

Imagine standing waist-deep in Alaska's icy waters, gripping a giant round net on a five-foot-long pole. The sun hangs low in the sky, refusing to set, and you're surrounded by the chatter of families, the hiss of camp stoves, and the sound of laughter carrying over the river. Then you finally feel that tug on your net, which you heave out of the water, and claim your shining, silver prize—a wild Alaskan salmon. That's dipnetting.

Reserved exclusively for Alaskan residents (who have lived in the state for at least one full year), this fishing method involves using long-handled nets to catch salmon as they migrate upriver to spawn. It's an experience that requires little skill but lots of patience and luck. Some days, the fish are so plentiful it feels like you can scoop them up by the dozen. On other days, it's hours of standing in the frigid water, waiting for that one perfect moment.

KENAI SOUTH BEACH

WHAT: The mouth of the famous Kenai River

WHERE: End of Old Cannery Rd., Kenai

COST: Free to visit

PRO TIP: On a clear day you can see five volcanoes from this beach.

For many, it's the highlight of the summer, a time when entire families hit the river, hoping to land enough salmon to fill their freezers for the long winter ahead. Unlike most fishing methods, dipnetting is a communal event. The riverbanks along the Kenai, Kasilof, and Copper Rivers are packed with families camping out in tents or RVs, cooking up freshly caught fish and swapping stories around the campfire.

While dipnetting is a fun and exciting way to gather food, it's also highly regulated to make sure fish populations stay healthy. Each household is limited to how many fish they

can catch, and the rules vary depending on the river and the type of salmon. And when returns are poor, rivers close to the practice—it's part of Fish and Game's strategy to keep the populations sustainable for future generations.

Out-of-staters aren't allowed to dipnet (and Alaska Fish and Game is diligent about checking permits, so don't try), but it's still a fun spectacle to watch if you're in the area.

TRUSTY *TUSTY*

How does one get to some of the most remote parts of the Aleutian Islands?

DUTCH HARBOR FERRY TERMINAL

WHAT: The easternmost terminal of the Alaska Marine Highway System

WHERE: 1503 Ballyhoo Rd., Unalaska

COST: Prices of ferry rides vary.

PRO TIP: Travel times between destinations can be long, with some communities over 24 hours apart. Be prepared for extended journeys, and bring items to entertain yourself.

In a land where wilderness reigns and roads can be scarce, the Alaska Marine Highway System, a state-run ferry network, serves as a vital lifeline for locals in more than 30 coastal communities, and it is a unique way for travelers to soak in stunning coastal vistas, like dizzying fjords, dense forests, and glacial ice fields.

Chances are, if you're hitching an aquatic ride along the lesser-visited Aleutian Island Chain, your steed will be the M/V *Tustumena*, a 290-foot-long vessel that can hold 220 passengers, affectionately nicknamed "Trusty *Tusty*." Having been in the fleet since 1964, it's the

oldest of the Alaska Marine Highway Systems ships and has a no-frills, utilitarian charm.

While cabins are available, many passengers set up camp in the solarium or on the ferry's deck, sleeping in tents or sleeping bags under the midnight sun. The workhorse of a ferry is designed for long-haul travel, offering basic but comfortable amenities, including a cafeteria and lounges. Whales, sea otters, puffins, and eagles are common sightings from the deck. You might even catch a glimpse of a bear lumbering along the shoreline or a pod of orcas breaching in the distance.

It's a slower, more immersive way to explore the 49th state, allowing you to visit the small towns, like Cignik, Sand Point, King Cove, Cold Bay, False Pass, and Akutan, that would otherwise be inaccessible. The entire route, stretching from Seldovia to Dutch Harbor, is roughly 900 miles, and most of those aboard ride *Tusty* both ways. For them, it's about the adventure.

The *Tustumena*'s reputation as "trusty" comes from its reliability in navigating some of the state's roughest waters, including the notoriously challenging Bering Sea.

STUCK IN THE MIDDLE

How did the town of McCarthy end up in the middle of the largest national park in the country?

McCarthy, Alaska, is arguably one of the most unique towns in America. It's situated smack-dab in the middle of a 13.2-million-acre national park.

When copper was discovered in the area at the beginning of the 1900s, the town of Kennicott and the Kennecott Mines (spelled differently due to a clerical error) sprung up around the deposits and drew workers from across the country with the promise of opportunities and wealth.

The mine needed a service town, and that's where McCarthy came into the picture. While Kennicott itself was a strictly controlled company town with no saloons, brothels, or gambling allowed, McCarthy quickly established itself as a place where miners and workers could blow off a bit of steam. Just five miles down the road from the mine, McCarthy became the site of bars, hotels, dance halls, and other businesses catering to the miners.

However, when the ore was depleted, the mines were abandoned and both Kennicott and McCarthy became ghost towns. For decades, McCarthy lay in near ruin, and its remote location—accessible only by small planes or a perilous gravel road—kept it off the beaten path for most travelers. It might have stayed that way, a relic of a bygone era, if not for the establishment of Wrangell-St. Elias National Park and Preserve in 1980. McCarthy's rebirth as a gateway to the park slowly began.

McCarthy's Golden Saloon is the only saloon in a United States national park. It's the best (and only) place in town for nightlife.

Photos courtesy of Take Aim Photography

MA JOHNSON'S HISTORICAL HOTEL

WHAT: A boardinghouse turned hotel

WHERE: 100 Kennicott Ave., McCarthy

COST: Room rates vary.

PRO TIP: The hotel has 20 unique rooms, each with period pieces from McCarthy's heyday, such as original bed frames, handmade quilts, and artifacts from the town's history.

Over time, the town attracted residents (there are currently roughly 100 people living in the former ghost town) who valued its seclusion and history. In the last few decades, the old saloons, shops, and hotels were revitalized and new outposts for outdoor guiding companies and eateries sprung up. While much has changed, McCarthy retains its identity as a place where time moves a little slower, and the grandeur of the wilderness looms large.

THE TOUGHEST 5K

What makes the Mount Marathon Race one of the most challenging races out there?

For competitors, the namesake peak of the Mount Marathon Race stands as both the arena and the opponent. It's the reason the race is frequently called the Toughest 5K on Earth.

Every year on the Fourth of July, competitors run from downtown Seward to the top of the mountain and back. The ascent is a relentless scramble up loose rock, mud, and shale, with runners often resorting to hands-and-knees crawling on the steepest sections. All told, racers gain 3,022 feet of elevation in a single .9-mile section. Once they reach the summit, the real test begins: a breakneck descent where agility, balance, and sheer bravery are key. Many describe the downhill as more dangerous than the climb, with the loose gravel turning the mountain into a slippery gauntlet. Many people say if you're not bleeding by the time you finish, you didn't try hard enough.

The origins of the Mount Marathon Race date back to 1915, and like many great Alaskan stories, it began with a barroom bet. As legend has it, two men argued over whether it was possible to ascend and descend the mountain in less than an hour. To settle the debate, they staged the first race. The winning racer finished in 1 hour and 2 minutes. Today, the fastest-ever time is 40 minutes, 37 seconds. The winner gets a trophy, bragging rights, and (should they want

MOUNT MARATHON RACE

WHAT: The oldest mountain race in North America

WHERE: Seward

COST: Free to watch; competing costs a fee.

PRO TIP: Scout the course beforehand, especially if you're a first-time participant. While it may seem straightforward, the route has some tricky sections, particularly during the descent, where knowing the terrain can make all the difference.

to put themselves through it again) free entry into future Mount Marathon Races.

It's possible to hike Mount Marathon any day of the year and mere mortals might consider the (slightly) easier Jeep Trail to the top. There's no trophy for reaching the summit—the prize is a 360-degree panorama of the Kenai Peninsula's towering peaks and the shimmering expanse of Resurrection Bay.

Over the decades, the race has grown from a quirky local event to an internationally recognized competition that draws elite athletes from around the globe.

ALASKA'S TWO ELEPHANTS

Why aren't there elephants in Alaska now?

The story of how the Alaska Zoo started begins with a toilet paper contest.

In 1966, Crown Zellerbach offered a prize of $3,000 or a baby elephant to whichever grocery store sold the most of its Chiffon Tissue. When Jack Snyder, a grocery store owner in Fairbanks, won, he surprised the company by choosing the pachyderm.

ALASKA ZOO

WHAT: A zoo with more than 100 birds and 50 species of mammals

WHERE: 4731 O'Malley Rd., Anchorage

COST: Varies

PRO TIP: During the summer, the zoo offers tours and animal-feeding experiences.

Soon Annabelle the Asian elephant was living in Alaska, first at a university farm in Fairbanks and then Diamond H Horse Ranch in Anchorage. The latter was owned by Sammye Seawell, who Snyder eventually gave the elephant to.

Seawell was known for adopting animals in need—before Annabelle, she adopted an orphaned harbor seal she named Oley. And later, state wildlife officials asked her to take in two more orphans: Tuffy the black bear and Sally the Arctic fox. Eventually, Seawell decided if she wanted to continue to provide homes for orphaned and injured wildlife, she'd need to start a zoo. On August 2, 1969, the Alaska Zoo opened its gates to visitors.

In 1983, a one-year-old African elephant named Maggie was brought in to be Annabelle's companion. Sadly, in December 1997, Annabelle had to be euthanized, as an infection had spread into her bones and bloodstream. Seawell stroked her trunk in her final moments.

Photo courtesy of Alaska Zoo

Because the Alaska Zoo had since adopted a policy to allow only animals native to Alaska, Maggie couldn't get a companion. After much public outcry, it was decided she'd be sent to the Performing Animal Welfare Society Wildlife Sanctuary near Sacramento (where she stayed until her passing in 2021). In November 2007, Maggie boarded one of the largest cargo jets ever made, on loan from the US Air Force, and flew from Elmendorf Air Force Base in Anchorage to the sanctuary. Her friend Bob Barker paid for her flight.

In the '90s, Annabelle was taught to paint as a form of enrichment—her paintings sold for hundreds of dollars and her paintbrush is still on display in the zoo's gift shop.

SOURCES

Stubbs, Talkeetna's Fictitious Feline Mayor
edition.cnn.com/2017/07/23/us/mayor-cat-stubbs-dies-at-20/index.html

smithsonianmag.com/smart-news/beloved-alaskan-cat-mayor-dies-180964188/

Betting on Ice
nenanaakiceclassic.com/

atlasobscura.com/articles/alaska-ice-lottery-nenana

White Alice
alaska.org/detail/anvil-mountain-white-alice-antennas-viewpoint

tile.loc.gov/storage-services/master/pnp/habshaer/ak/ak0200/ak0213/data/ak0213data.pdf

beringstraits.com/historical-spotlight-white-alice/

Sourdough
atlasobscura.com/articles/what-is-sourdough-alaska

uaf.edu/ces/publications/database/food/files/pdfs/FNH-00061-Sourdough.pdf

A MacGyvered Car
fountainheadmuseum.com/fountainheadauto/tag/1905+Sheldon+Car

alaskamagazine.com/authentic-alaska/30-second-reads/the-first-car-in-alaska-is-still-on-display/

Spirit Houses
nmfh.org/tiny-spirit-houses-of-eklutna/

alaska.org/detail/eklutna-village

alaskasnewssource.com/2022/06/08/roadtrippin-2022-preserving-family-history-through-spirit-houses-eklutna-historical-park/

Alaska's Signature Beverage
chowhound.com/recipes/duck-fart-13717/

anchoragepress.com/food_and_drink/drink-of-the-week-the-duck-fart-at-peanut-farm/article_92ad7c86-5bad-11e9-b518-ab5996f29980.html

Star, Anchorage's Unofficial Mascot
adn.com/alaska-news/anchorage/2017/10/08/anchorages-iconic-star-the-reindeer-dies-at-age-15/

alaskapublic.org/2012/12/24/star-the-reindeer-brings-magic-to-downtown-anchorage/

The Parking Fairies
adn.com/alaska-life/2020/01/06/the-anchorage-parking-fairies-how-a-75-ticket-started-a-movement/

Porta Potty Pushing
furrondy.net/events/outhouse-races/

anchorage.net/winter/events/fur-rondy/

smithsonianmag.com/travel/inside-worlds-largest-outhouse-race-180971579/

Of Bears and Salmon
nps.gov/katm/index.htm

Gold and Good Humor
archive.is/7LQhM

On Dasher, On Dancer
furrondy.net/events/running-of-the-reindeer/

alaska.org/detail/running-of-the-reindeer

reindeerfarm.com/

Lend Me Some Sugar: I Am Your Neighbor
npr.org/2015/01/18/378162264/welcome-to-whittier-alaska-a-community-under-one-roof

edition.cnn.com/interactive/2015/07/us/whittier-alaska-american-story/

Roots Up
thealaskafrontier.com/upside-down-trees-in-alaska/

glaciergardens.com/

America's Last Whistle-Stop Train
alaskarailroad.com/

npr.org/2011/09/19/140506015/into-the-wild-alaskan-train-caters-to-the-intrepid

A True Melting Pot
census.gov/content/dam/Census/library/stories/2024/01/racial-ethnic-diversity-neighborhoods/figure-1-racial-ethnic-diversity-neighborhoods.jpg

The Bar Fare of Choice
atlasobscura.com/foods/reindeer-dog-anchorage-alaska

Dr. Seuss House
alaska.org/detail/dr-seuss-house

atlasobscura.com/places/dr-seuss-house-aka-the-goose-creek-tower

One Part Bar, One Part Museum
koots.com/history

alaskapublic.org/2014/02/24/touring-an-iconic-anchorage-bar/

anchoragepress.com/news/end-of-an-era/article_88132165-c058-50ca-a742-9ca01da5d3fd.html

The Tale of Togo
nps.gov/people/togo.htm#:~:text=Named%20after%20Heihachiro%20Togo%2C%20a,cream%2C%20black%20and%20grey%20markings.

akc.org/expert-advice/news/togo-siberian-husky-sled-dog-hero-of-1925/

A Village Frozen in Time
eater.com/23204115/alaska-history-russia-old-believer-samovar

An Abandoned Mine
nps.gov/wrst/learn/historyculture/kennecott-mines-national-historic-landmark.htm

alaska.org/detail/kennicott-mine-ghost-town-walking-tour

Shame on You
alaskahistoricalsociety.org/about-ahs/special-projects/150treaty/150th-resource-library/new-articles/the-seward-shame-pole-countering-alaskas-sesquicentennial/

mesocosm.net/2012/06/01/the-tlingit-the-raven-and-a-shame-pole-for-exxon/

juneauempire.com/news/gut-fish-not-alaska-totem-pole-ridicules-trump-and-dunleavy/

Alaska, Florida
npr.org/sections/thesalt/2016/03/29/469957638/baked-alaska-a-creation-story-shrouded-in-mystery

tastingtable.com/990115/the-origin-story-of-the-baked-alaska

Operation Breakthrough
livescience.com/31125-real-big-miracle-story.html

timesmachine.nytimes.com/timesmachine/1988/10/18/430388.html?pageNumber=18

encountersalaska.com/bowhead-whaling#:~:text=In%201854%2C%20the%20first%20commercial,Inupiat%20and%20European%2FAmerican%20whalers

Be Kind: Rewind
adn.com/business-economy/2018/07/12/the-last-two-blockbuster-stores-in-alaska-are-set-to-close

theweek.com/speedreads/771153/thanks-john-oliver-lone-blockbuster-video-alaska-displaying-russell-crowes-jockstrap

A Side of Ranch
ediblealaska.ediblecommunities.com/recipes/made-alaska-ranch-dressing

Launched from the Sky on the Fourth of July
roadtrippers.com/magazine/alaska-car-launch

alaskasnewssource.com/video/2024/07/05/alaskans-celebrate-fourth-july-with-signature-car-launch

The Flower Man Lives On
roadtrippers.com/magazine/flower-man-anchorage

anchoragepress.com/news/bed-of-roses-a-community-remembers-john-jilwan/article_9ad9ed5a-f21e-11ea-aadd-6fab83de0dd8.html

Juneau's Most Famous Dog
traveljuneau.com/discover-juneau/history/pasty-ann-canine-greeter

patsyann.com

A Remote Homestead
alaska.org/detail/don-sheldon-mountain-house

sheldonchalet.com

architecturaldigest.com/story/sheldon-chalet

On the Half-Shell
architecturaldigest.com/story/sheldon-chalet

It's Hammer Time
hammermuseum.org/history

visithaines.com/listing/the-hammer-museum/265

Eight Gold Stars in a Blue Sky
britannica.com/topic/flag-of-Alaska

alaskahistoricalsociety.org/discover-alaska/kids-page/benny-benson-an-alaska-kid-who-made-history

Sleeping Lady
alaska.org/detail/mount-susitna

muni.org/Departments/health/PHIP/safepubs/vol%201%202006%20native%20guide%20for%20web.pdf

alaskavipclub.com/p/anchorage-facts-and-history-550

Cowabunga, Dude
alaska.org/advice/alaska-bore-tide

girdwood.com/girdwood-turnagain-arm-bore-tide-what-when-where-why-and-who

The Bawdy Past of Creek Street
creekstreetketchikan.com

experienceketchikan.com/creek-street-ketchikan.html

All Aboard and Going Nowhere
alaska.org/detail/the-last-train-to-nowhere

Spinning a Yarn
alaskayaks.com

An Unlikely Outpost
lastfrontierheli.com/news/gettin-hyderized-in-alaska

travelalaska.com/destinations/cities-towns/hyder

Hoot, Howl, Bugle, and Roar
alaskawildlife.org

Wilderness Woman
talkeetnabachelors.com/wilderness

alaskavisit.com/blog/post/wilderness-woman-bachelor-auction

A Chocolate Cascade
akwildberry.com/about-us/worlds-largest-chocolate-falls

worldrecordacademy.org/2023/11/worlds-largest-chocolate-waterfall-world-record-in-anchorage-alaska-423560

roadsideamerica.com/tip/16419

Bunking Down in History
nationalgeographic.com/travel/article/alaskas-rugged-roadhouses-serve-up-hospitality-and-history

lodgeatblackrapids.com/historic-roadhouse-restoration-project

Ice, Ice Baby
usgs.gov/faqs/how-many-glaciers-currently-exist-alaska

alaska.org/advice/glaciers-in-alaska

Blue Babe
uaf.edu/museum/press/spotlight/blue-babe

atlasobscura.com/articles/ancient-bison-stew-blue-babe-alaska

books.google.com/books?-id=KOzYAgAAQBAJ&pg=PA324&lpg=PA324&dq=bjorn+kurten+bison+stew&source=bl&ots=RZBp2v7I_Q&sig=_3giZ4YQOP_uPWpID4xSifDBvNA&hl=en&sa=X&ved=0ahUKEwj3oMezxPbYAhU-GSt8KHRzFDGkQ6AEITTAK#v=onepage&q=bjorn%20kurten%20bison%20stew&f=false

Here Comes the (Midnight) Sun
travelalaska.com/explore-alaska/articles/midnight-sun-alaska

On the Rocks
chenahotsprings.com/aurora-ice-museum

World-Traveling Totems
nps.gov/sitk/learn/historyculture/the-missing-poles.htm

nps.gov/sitk/index.htm

The Only Way Out Is Through It
whittieralaska.gov/tunnel

whittieralaska.gov/tunnel

Beware the Crab
chroniclingamerica.loc.gov/lccn/sn84026749/1923-07-30/ed-1/seq-1/#date1=1923&index=0&rows=20&words=crab+meat+poisoning&searchType=basic&sequence=0&state=&date2=1923&proxtext=%22crab+meat+poisoning%22+&y=1-9&x=10&dateFilterType=yearRange&page=1

smithsonianmag.com/history/why-president-warren-g-hardings-sudden-death-sparked-rumors-of-murder-and-suicide-180982626/

alaska.org/detail/fairview-inn

alaskahistoricalsociety.org/president-hardings-voyage-of-understanding-june-1923/

Four-Legged National Park Rangers
smithsonianmag.com/travel/how-denali-national-parks-sled-dogs-prepare-for-winter-180976550/

nps.gov/dena/planyourvisit/kennels.htm

Cherry, Pumpkin, or Lemon Meringue
atlasobscura.com/articles/alaska-sled-dog-race

Hello, Dolly
redonion1898.com/

alaska.org/detail/red-onion-saloon

Don't Forget Socks
travelalaska.com/destinations/cities-towns/coldfoot

coldfootcamp.com/

Dollar Bills and Lime Wedges
alaskasnewssource.com/2022/06/07/roadtrippin-2022-history-behind-salty-dawg-saloon/

saltydawgsaloon.com/

homeralaska.org/listing/salty-dawg-saloon/64/

Bus 142
outsideonline.com/outdoor-adventure/exploration-survival/chris-mccandless-into-the-wild-bus-142-alaska/

nytimes.com/2020/06/19/us/into-the-wild-bus-removed.html

A Town Built on Cheer
santaclaushouse.com/about.asp

So Close, Yet So Far
snopes.com/fact-check/sarah-palin-russia-house/

nps.gov/anch/learn/historyculture/how-close-is-alaska-to-russia.htm#:~:text=However%2C%20in%20the%20body%20of,is%20owned%20by%20the%20US.

A Lunar Landscape on Earth
nps.gov/katm/index.htm

nps.gov/katm/planyourvisit/exploring-the-valley-of-ten-thousand-smokes.htm

Alaska's Favorite Cracker
atlasobscura.com/articles/why-alaskans-still-eat-hardtack

sitnews.us/Kiffer/PilotBread/061812_pilot_bread.html

An Architectural Oddity
alaskapublic.org/2023/06/27/the-parks-highway-igloos-being-renovated-to-sell-booze/

There's Gold in Those Hills
travelalaska.com/destinations/parks-public-lands/independence-mine-state-historical-park#:~:text=6%2C000%20feet%20tall.-,HISTORY,hardrock%20gold%20mine%20in%20Alaska.

dnr.alaska.gov/parks/aspunits/matsu/indepmineshp.htm

Shake, Rattle, and Roll
atlasobscura.com/places/earthquake-park-anchorage-alaska

seismic.alaska.gov/earthquake-risk.html

Burning Man, Alaska Style
sbnation.com/longform/2014/7/23/5923357/arctic-man-alaska-ski-race-profile#4097098

theguardian.com/us-news/2016/apr/24/arctic-man-burning-man-festival-alaska-ski-snowmobile-race

Cultural Preservation in a Modern Context
alaskanative.net/

alaska.org/detail/alaska-native-heritage-center

Up, Up, and Away
dot.alaska.gov/stwdav/

alaskaairmuseum.org/

An Extra Serving of Vegetables
alaskastatefair.org/site/giant-fruit-vegetable-records/

adn.com/alaska-life/2019/08/28/theres-a-new-state-record-for-giant-pumpkins/

Fish On!
thebaitshackak.com/events/2021-slamn-salmn-derby

adfg.alaska.gov/sf/FishingReports/index.cfm?ADFG=R2.summary&Area_key=1&RecordID=5

Nature's Light Show
alaskatours.com/alaska-stories/alaskaa-northern-lights-myths-legends-and-science/

alaska.org/things-to-do/northern-lights-viewing#:~:text=Fairbanks%20and%20points%20north%20are,arc%20above%20the%20Alaska%20Range.

In Celebration of Slush
alaska.org/detail/alyeska-slush-cup

alyeskaresort.com/events/spring-carnival/

Rudolph and All His Friends
runningreindeer.com/

Icy What You Did There
icealaska.com/

opb.org/article/2023/12/07/from-oregon-to-alaska-an-ice-sculpting-odyssey/

explorefairbanks.com/event/world-ice-art-championships-2024/7928/

Alone In the Wilderness
nationalparked.com/gates-of-the-arctic/visitation-statistics

nps.gov/gaar/learn/what-is-gates-of-the-arctic.htm#:~:text=The%20landscape%20is%20covered%20by,bears%20also%20inhabit%20the%20land.

Three Bears
anchorage.net/plan-your-trip/things-to-know/frequently-asked-alaska-travel-questions/where-can-i-see-polar-bears/

alaskazoo.org/polar-bear-camera#:~:text=Welcome%20to%20the%20Alaska%20Zoo's,full%20story%20and%20release%20here.

travelalaska.com/explore-alaska/articles/how-to-view-alaska-bears

adfg.alaska.gov/index.cfm?adfg=polarbear.main

Birds of a Feather
baldeagles.org/

visithaines.com/events/annual-events/alaska-bald-eagle-festival/

Flippers and Fins
alaskasealife.org/

Caribou and Sand Dunes
npshistory.com/publications/kova/index.htm#:~:text=Its%20valley%20

provides%20important%20fall,on%20their%20extensive%20annual%20migrations.

sciencenews.org/article/caribou-migrate-farther-than-any-other-known-land-animal#:~:text=Some%20herds%20of%20caribou%20migrate,breeding%20grounds%20and%20back%20again.

nps.gov/kova/blogs/the-great-kobuk-sand-dunes-a-cloudy-and-warming-crystal-ball-for-mars.htm

All Caught Up

theguardian.com/environment/2020/aug/20/fish-free-for-all-alaskans-sockeye-salmon

alaskapublic.org/2024/07/26/its-dipnetting-season-and-alaskans-say-the-annual-tradition-is-about-more-than-just-filling-their-freezers/

Trusty *Tusty*

adn.com/we-alaskans/article/900-mile-trip-trusty-tusty-both-cruise-ship-and-greyhound-bus/2015/08/09/

Stuck In the Middle

nps.gov/wrst/index.htm

The Toughest 5K

alaska.org/detail/mount-marathon-race-route

mountmarathon.com/for-racer/racer-faq/#:~:text=The%20winner%20gets%20a%20trophy,with%20the%20Mount%20Marathon%20Race.

Alaska's Two Elephants

alaskazoo.org/what-we-do

adn.com/alaska-life/2020/12/06/how-a-1960s-publicity-stunt-landed-a-baby-elephant-named-annabelle-in-alaska/

myemail.constantcontact.com/PRESS-RELEASE---Performing-Animal-Welfare-Society-Announces-Death-of-African-Elephant-Maggie.html?soid=1101778242429&aid=IN1QwmfO3mg

INDEX

49th State Brewing, 73, 117
Alaska Aviation Museum, 136–137
Alaska Bald Eagle Festival, 154
Alaska Chilkat Bald Eagle Preserve, 154
Alaska Marine Highway System, 162–163
Alaska Native, 34–36, 134–135
Alaska Native Heritage Center, 134–135
Alaska Purchase, 50
Alaska Railroad, 32–33, 38, 104
Alaska SeaLife Center, 156–157
Alaska State Fair, 138
Alaska state flag, 70
Alaska State Museum, 70
Alaska Wildberry Products, 88–89
Alaska Wildlife Conservation Center, 84
Alaska Zoo, 152, 168–169
Aleutian Islands, 162
Alyeska Resort, 144–145
American Bald Eagle Foundation, 154–155
Anaktuvuk Pass Ranger Station, 150
Anchorage, 12, 15, 15–20, 26, 32–37, 40, 51, 54–55, 57, 60, 72–74, 88, 97, 108, 119, 124, 130–131, 134–136, 140, 152, 168–169
Anton Anderson Memorial Tunnel, 102
Arctic, 52–53, 80–81, 126, 150–151, 158, 168
Arctic Circle, 96, 112, 150, 152
Arctic Man, 132–133
Arctic National Wildlife Refuge, 113
Athabascan, 12, 134, 142
aurora borealis, 142
Aurora Ice Museum, 98–99
Bachelor Ball, 86
Baked Alaska, 50–51
bald eagle, 30, 154–155
Balto, 42
bear (brown, black, and polar), 22–23, 38, 82, 84, 101, 106, 152–153, 163, 168
Begich Towers Condominium, 28
Beluga Point, 74
Benny Benson, 70
Bering Land Bridge National Preserve, 153
Bering Sea, 42–43
Big Dipper, 71
Blockbuster, 54–55
Blue Babe, 94–95
bore tide, 74–75
Brooks Camp, 23, 123
Brooks Falls, 22–23, 123
Brooks Mountain Range, 112
Brooks River, 22
brothel, 77, 110–111
bus, 142, 116–117
bush pilot, 64–65, 136
Cantwell, 136
Cape Krusenstern National Monument, 153, 158
caribou, 38, 99, 106, 146, 150, 158–159
Chena Hot Springs, 98, 143
Chicken, 24–25
Chicken Gold Camp, 25
Chilkoot Charlie's, 40
Chitina, 46
chocolate waterfall, 88

Chugach Mountains, 28, 84
Coldfoot, 112–113
Cold War, 6, 120
Cordova, 49, 93
crab, 14, 40, 66, 104
Creek Street, 76–77
Dall sheep, 38
Deadliest Catch, 14
Denali, 3, 33, 38, 64–65, 93, 105–107, 116, 126
Denali National Park, 64, 106–107, 116, 126
Diomede Islands (Big and Little), 120–121
diphtheria, 42
dipnetting, 160
Dolly's House Museum, 77
Dr. Seuss House, 38
Duck Fart Shot, 14–15
Dutch Harbor, 14, 162–163
earthquake, 90, 130–131
Earthquake Park, 130–131
Eklutna, 12
Eklutna Historical Park, 12
Fairbanks, 10–11, 32, 39, 90, 94, 97–98, 116–117, 142–143, 146, 148–149, 168
Fairbanks Ice Museum, 149
Fairview Inn, 87, 104–105
Flower Man, 60
Flower Towers, 30–31
Fountainhead Antique Auto Museum, 11
Fourth of July, 58, 166
Fur Rendezvous, 17, 20
Gates of the Arctic National Park, 113, 150–151
ghost town, 1, 46, 164
Girdwood, 84, 144–145
glacier, 46, 58, 64–65, 92–93, 150, 158
Glacier Gardens Rainforest Adventure, 30
Glacier Inn, 83
Glacier View Car Launch, 58
gold rush, 1, 8, 24, 78, 82, 110, 112
Goose Creek Tower, 38
Haida, 100
Haines, 68–69, 154–155
halibut, 44, 66, 114
Hammer Museum, 1, 68–69
Harding, Warren G., President, 104
Homer, 88, 114–115
homestead, 33, 64–65
Hump Island Oyster Co., 66
Hurricane Gulch, 33
husky, 16
Hyder, 82–83
Ice Alaska, 148
Iditarod Sled Dog Race, 26, 108
Iditarod Headquarters, 42
Igloo City, 126–127
Independence Mine State Historical Park, 128
Indigenous, 10, 16, 48, 72, 94, 100, 120, 134–135, 142
Into the Wild, 85, 116–117
Iñupiat, 52–53, 96, 120, 134, 142, 159
Iñupiat Heritage Center, 52
Jilwan, Jean, 60–61
Juneau, 32, 62–63, 88, 93
Kaasen, Gunnar, 42
Kachemak Bay, 114
Katmai National Park, 22–23, 122–123, 158
Kenai, 160
Kenai Peninsula, 32, 167

Kennecott Mines, 47
Kennecott Mines National Historic Landmark, 46
Kennicott, 46–47, 165
Ketchikan, 48, 66, 76–77
king salmon, 23, 140
Klondike Gold Rush, 8, 110
Kobuk Valley National Park, 150, 158
Kodiak, 122, 131
Koot's, 40
Kotzebue, 84, 158
Lake Hood, 137
Last Train to Nowhere, 78
Linny Pacillo Parking Garage, 18
Ma Johnson's Historical Hotel, 165
McCandless, Chris, 116
McCarthy, 164–165
Mendenhall Glacier, 93
midnight sun, 1, 96–97, 163
mine, 46–47, 68, 90, 94, 128–129, 164
moose, 36, 84–85, 108, 124, 143, 147
Moose's Tooth Pub & Pizzeria, 57
Mount Marathon, 166–167
Mount Susitna, 72–73
museum, 1, 10–11, 40, 52, 68–70, 77, 90, 94–95, 98–100, 110–111, 117, 136–137, 149, 155
Museum of the North, 10, 94–95, 117
musher, 42, 108–109
musk ox, 80–81, 147, 150
Musk Ox Farm, 81
M/V *Tustumena*, 162
Nagley's Store, 2
NASA, 22, 123, 159
Nenana Ice Classic, 4–5
New Sagaya City Market, 34
Nikolaevsk, 44–45
Nome, 6, 26, 42, 78, 97
Nomehenge, 6
northern lights, 65, 99, 113, 142–143
North Pole, 118–119
Northwest Arctic Heritage Center, 158
Outhouse Race, 20
oyster, 66–67
Pancho's Villa, 61
Palmer, 16, 81, 138, 147
Parking Fairies, 18–19
park ranger, 46, 106, 150
Patsy Ann, 62–63
Peanut Farm, 15
pie, 108–109
Point Barrow, 96–97
Prohibition, 76–77
Prince William Sound, 30, 103
ptarmigan, 24, 86
qiviut, 80–81
ranch dressing, 56–57
Red Onion Saloon, 110–111
reindeer, 16–17, 26–27, 36–37, 118, 146–147
Reindeer Farm, 16
reindeer hot dog, 36–37
Resurrection Bay, 156, 167
roadhouse, 8, 90–91
Running of the Reindeer, 26
Running Reindeer Ranch, 146
Russian Orthodox, 12, 41, 44
Russian Old Believers, 44
Ruth Glacier, 64, 93
Sailor Boy Pilot Bread, 124–125

salmon, 22–24, 44, 66, 76, 82, 114, 124, 140, 143, 154, 160–161
Salty Dawg Saloon, 114–115
Samovar Cafe, 45
Santa, 21, 118–119
Santa Claus House, 118–119
Saxman Totem Park, 48
Seppala, Leonhard, 42–43
Seward, 32, 70, 156–157, 166–167
Seward Highway, 15, 57, 74, 84
Seward, William H., 48
shame pole, 48–49
Sheldon, Bobby, 10
Sheldon Chalet, 65
Sheldon, Don, 64
Ship Creek, 140–141
Sitka, 49, 100
Sitka National Historical Park, 100
Skagway, 10, 110–111
sled dog, 20, 62, 106–108
Sleeping Lady, 72
Slush Cup, 144–145
snow, 26, 29, 65, 99, 106, 118, 126, 132, 144, 146, 151, 158
snowmachine, 86, 132
sourdough, 1, 8–9
spawn, 22, 66, 77, 160
Spenard, 40, 60
speakeasy, 76
spirit houses, 12–13
Star the Reindeer, 16–17
statehood, 7, 40, 70, 100
steppe bison, 94
Sterling Highway, 44
Stubbs, 2–3
subsistence food, 36
surfing, 74
Sutton, 58
Talkeetna, 2–3, 8–9, 33, 38, 86–87, 90, 104
Talkeetna Roadhouse, 8, 90
Tia's Gourmet Sausages and Hotdogs, 36
Tlingit, 69, 100, 134
Togo, 42–43
Tongass National Forest, 30, 82
totem pole, 48, 100
Trans-Alaska Pipeline, 113
Trusty *Tusty*, 162–163
tundra, 78, 80, 132, 152, 158
Turnagain Arm, 74–75
Utqiagvik, 52–53, 96, 152–153
Valdez, 11, 131
Valdez Trail, 11
Valley of Ten Thousand Smokes, 22
Wasilla, 42
whale, 52–53, 163
Whistle-Stop, 32–33
White Alice, 6–7
Whittier, 28–29, 102–103
Wild Scoops, 51
Wilderness Woman competition, 86–87
Willow, 38, 108
World's Fair, 100
World Ice Art Championships, 148
World War II, 44, 102, 110, 136
Wrangell-St. Elias National Park, 46, 164

Photo courtesy of Frank Flavin

Denali from Stony Overlook
Photo courtesy of the National Park Service